THE WIDOW-MAKER HEART ATTACK AT AGE 48

Written by a Heart Attack Survivor for a
Heart Attack Survivor and Their Loved Ones

Patrick J. Fox

authorHOUSE®

AuthorHouse™
1663 Liberty Drive
Bloomington, IN 47403
www.authorhouse.com
Phone: 833-262-8899

Published by AuthorHouse 06/25/2022

ISBN: 978-1-4389-6279-5 (sc)
ISBN: 978-1-4389-6280-1 (hc)
ISBN: 978-1-4389-6281-8 (e)

Library of Congress Control Number: 2009904347

Print information available on the last page.

www.widowmakerheartattack.com

This book is printed on acid-free paper.

DEDICATION

This book is dedicated to my entire family and all my friends. If it were not for their support and prayers I would not be here today. To all who are part of Christ Lutheran Church in Belvidere, Illinois, and all the administrators, faculty, staff, and students at Rockford East High School …

Thank you!

CONTENTS

Walt Disney World
Guest Relations
P.O. Box 1000
Lake Buena Vista, Florida 32830

To Whom It May Concern:

Hello my name is Brandon Fox; I am a Walt Disney World Cast Member in the entertainment department. I started in the Company in the College Program and I have now gone seasonal. I even came down and worked during my college spring break. I bought this shirt for my father during my short work period during spring break (which is enclosed in package).

I arrived back home on March 24th and on the morning of March 31st my father, Patrick Fox woke me up and told me that he was ironing his favorite shirt to wear to work. I said; "Ok Dad, I don't have to be up for another hour." Then he thought it was appropriate to wake me up again and show me how good it looked. My father loves Disney and he was the reason I started to work in the company. He loves everything that he has from Disney; books, clothing, movies, etc.

Around 9:30 that morning my father was at work as a teacher at a high school and was feeling some back pain but he tried toughing it out. The pain became too much to handle and the school had to call an ambulance. It turns out my father was having a massive heart attack and was minutes from passing away. While the paramedics were trying to revive him he was dreading that they had to cut his shirt. After shocking him six times to keep him alive and implanting a stent in his heart they were able to revive him. After he woke up from surgery and become aware of his surroundings, he asked for the Chicago Cubs home opener game on TV and his copy of the SpectroMagic Compact Disc (CD). My father has the SpectroMagic CD on repeat; it is all he listens to in his car. He says that the music inspires him to heal.

I am writing this in an effort to help my father. I am requesting the possibility that you could refund the shirt and by chance send him a replacement. Thank you for taking the time to read this letter. The magic of Disney and his passion for Disney is what continues to help my father grow stronger. My Dad, Patrick Fox believes strongly in the Disney Company. He sponsors Disney CareerStart recruiting days at East High School, in Rockford, Illinois, in hopes to create an opportunity for students who have very few options for a positive future. Even an acknowledgement of this letter and words of well wishes would truly brighten his life at this time when it is hard to be optimistic. Thanks again and have a magical day.

Sincerely,
Brandon Fox

To this day, I find myself reading my son's letter to the Disney Company on almost a daily basis. And to this day it reminds me that I did indeed go through a life-changing experience that some days I truly find difficult to believe.

INTRODUCTION

I have written this book in the hopes that my words and feelings might shed better light on the personal feelings, experiences, and changes in the life of a heart attack victim. In writing this book I can only hope that other families and loved ones facing the same devastating unfamiliar territory as mine did on March 31, 2008, might better be able to understand what the patient is going through and what loved ones might do to help the patient better deal with the difficult experience.

It is my intention that my experiences and corresponding words might also assist in making life just a little bit easier on the victim to better help the patient through the life-changing and emotional process of heart attack recovery.

This book is not meant to be a catchall for heart attack victims and their families. I have come to learn since my own heart attack the simple fact that all heart attacks are not created equal. I have had many good conversations with other heart attack victims since my own heart attack. I have found myself feeling jealous of those heart disease patients who were lucky enough to have warning signs and avoided the trauma and devastation of the dreaded heart attack all together.

The idea for this book came from my wife, daughter, and son as a therapeutic process for my recovery. In the days and months following my heart attack they were searching for as much information as possible to help them understand what I had been through, both medically and emotionally. They searched for books related to relatively young and healthy people having devastating heart attacks. Sadly, they found little or nothing on the subject, which is why I have decided to write this much-needed book.

While my family did not experience the heart attack themselves, they are nonetheless indirect victims. My wish in writing this book is that any family member of any heart attack victim might take some solace that they are not alone and that their day-to- day emotions are real and not to be ignored but rather learned from and grown upon.

I do not for one second think that I have come anywhere close to having experienced all the ups and downs related to a heart attack. On the other hand, I am happy and blessed to be in a position, I hope, to help those who are living through the same or a similar experience.

LIVING A DREAM LIFE

My life has been much like the script of any Disney movie. The beginning of my life script started in Huntington, West Virginia. I have been forever proud to tell people when asked that I was born in Huntington, West Virginia. I would truly love to visit there someday, but regretfully I don't remember anything about that city, as I moved from Huntington two years after my birth.

My most memorable years were spent in what I would call my unofficial "hometown," Leesburg, Indiana. Much like the TV show that most baby boomers grew up watching, Leesburg was my *Mayberry RFD*. The streets were brick and the residents mirrored in a positive light similar to the townspeople of Mayberry—Barney, Aunt Bee, Gomer, and Sheriff Andy—in their pleasant and small-town attitude.

I am sure that my memories of P.O. Box 7 in Leesburg might be a little distorted with time, but the late Mr. and Mrs. Smith will forever be a very bright and memorable part of my young life. My years in Leesburg with my two brothers, John (one year older) and

Jimmy (three years younger), and my two younger sisters, Kathy (two years younger) and finally Susie (six years younger), were in my fond memory very special years in the growth of our very close family. My memories of our family growing up in Leesburg and the special townspeople are of fun and are oriented around family.

We grew up decorating bikes to ride in the Fourth of July parade that would snake throughout the entire town. Perhaps my memories of Leesburg, Indiana, have something to do with my desire to move to Rock City, Illinois, where I currently reside. While no city can ever take the place of my memories of Leesburg, Indiana, in the late sixties, Rock City, Dakota, and Davis, Illinois certainly have been special.

It was during the Christmas holiday of 1969 that the Fox family took up roots in Leesburg and moved to Rockford, Illinois. My memories of the remaining years of elementary school at Gregory School were fun and very active years to say the least. My mom and dad were incredible, as they were as close to Superman and Superwoman as was humanly possible as they seemed to drop off five kids for basketball, baseball, football, Scouts, and friend get-togethers as only superheroes could accomplish.

I realized even in elementary school that when asked "what I wanted to do when I grew up" all I ever wanted to do was have my own business (entrepreneur; if I would have known that word then). As I lived through the high school life I learned early on that if I wanted to change things to be what I wanted I needed to be in a position to make things happen. I started by becoming an active part of the school yearbook and newspaper. In three years as yearbook and newspaper photographer, I met every teacher, administrator, and student who had any influence in making school decisions that could possibly impact in any way how much fun I or my fellow classmates had during our senior year. I would hazard to bet that most if not all of the seniors in 1978 at East High School had a very, very memorable senior year.

A big part of who I am today was derived from my active participation in high school sports. An anticipated four years of sports in the Rockford school district was cowardly halted due to the elimination of all extracurricular sports my junior year because of a tax referendum failure. The three years of active participation and the one year that was eliminated due to lame reasons have molded me more as an adult than anything else I have ever encountered.

The competitiveness I learned for the three years is something that has paid large dividends throughout my entire adult life. On the other side of the equation the anger of losing something that should have never been lost my junior year has provided a motivation to make change and not accept ineptness as an accepted norm.

The only good thing in a sea of bad moments my junior year at East when sports were eliminated was that it was during that summer that I volunteered to coach my first baseball team. It was then that I realized just how much I loved working with young kids, and not only just coaching them on the sport of baseball. I also realized that coaching was about much more than that, also influencing the character and opinions of the young people.

It was also during my junior year that I told myself that I wanted to define what the Rockford East (http://schools.rps205.com/east) class of 1978 would experience for better or worse. It was then that I decided to run for and win the election for senior class president. In the end, I don't think there were many in the class who thought our senior year was boring or dull.

One of my fondest memories was the relocation of many, many (okay … in excess of two hundred) real-estate "for sale" signs to the front yard of East High School. We are also remembered for the stacking of the flagpole in the front lawn of the school with used tires. This feat was something that for years previous classes had attempted via slingshot and other means. To finally accomplish the tires-over-the-flagpole "challenge" in a safe manner … we decided to just rent a crane and fill the flagpole to the top with old worn-out tires. Mission accomplished. *As a teacher at the same high school I must make the following statement: "Times have changed and I would not recommend these pranks to senior classes today."*

Without a doubt the most significant accomplishment of my entire four years at East High School was started during my junior year. Just after the Christmas holiday season my older brother John helped me get a job at a family soda parlor/restaurant. At the time the restaurant was called "The Last Straw" and was the most popular place for a good meal, soda jerks, and ice cream.

A special ice cream concoction was served by waitresses and soda jerks singing and running around the restaurant interior celebrating the purchase of the locally renowned "Fire Engine." It was during my employment at "The Last Straw" that the lucky meeting of an incredibly beautiful and delightful young woman named Jennifer occurred. My first date with that incredible young lady on Halloween of that year proved the first of many to come in the future. I ended up marrying that special girl six years later in 1982.

The other important experiences in my life arrived two years after my marriage in August of 1984 as we gave birth to the most beautiful daughter ever born on the planet: Stephanie. Then as if one miracle was not enough we were blessed with yet another child who just happened to be the most handsome baby boy ever born on earth in 1988: Brandon. Now, skipping forward nearly twenty years, both Stephanie and Brandon make me proud. Stephanie lives and works in Chicago, Illinois, while Brandon lives and works in Orlando, Florida.

Throughout my adult life I have followed most of my dreams. Shortly after graduating from Southern Illinois University at Carbondale, I started my first business: The Pride of Rockford Double Decker Bus Company. The Pride existed for nearly six years and only added fuel to my entrepreneurial passion. During the Pride's six-year life, I started and ended another business: The Good Times Theater. It was during this stage in my entrepreneurial career that I realized what I lacked on an educational level in order to be successful. It was then that I decided to pursue my Masters in Business Administration from the University of Phoenix.

25 years of saying "I Love You"

Celebrating our twenty-fifth anniversary at Tarryall River Ranch

I have always been driven to work with children since my junior year in high school at Rockford East High School. One of my most important and challenging life accomplishments was the founding of the Greater Rockford Little League. With the assistance of many incredible volunteers and the incredible assistance of the Rockford Park District, all with similar dreams and goals for young people, the Little League was established in Rockford, Illinois.

Nineteen years of coaching baseball, softball, football, and volleyball during my adult life provided me with incredible memories and lots of laughs watching young people develop emotionally but also physically as they participated in sports. The memories associated with coaching youth in Rockford and Dakota, Illinois, a small town west of Rockford, were indeed very special. The win-loss percentage I was able to accomplish may not have been the highest ever recorded in coaching, but nonetheless it helped make my life full and pretty outstanding.

Over the last six years I have been lucky enough to teach at East High School. At East I have truly enjoyed teaching business, computers, and newspaper and web design during my career.

One of my biggest accomplishments during my teaching career has been convincing the Walt Disney Company to recruit the students of East High School and other schools in northern Illinois for careers with the Walt Disney Company in Orlando, Florida. It was during the first year that I convinced Disney to recruit at East High School that I was able to provide a springboard for my son Brandon with his career at Disney. If it had not been for Disney recruiting at my high school I am not sure Brandon would have found Disney as a career.

Until March 31, 2008, my life was the best of all worlds. I lived in my dream log home and had two of the best kids that God ever put on earth and a wife with whom I had just celebrated twenty-five years of marriage, at Tarryall River Ranch (www.tarryallriverranch. com) in Lake George, Colorado. This was the same guest ranch where I had taken my family for a very special and memorable vacation ten years prior. It was during that incredible family vacation spent at Tarryall River Ranch that my dream of having a horse farm was re-fired. While we had indeed experienced special memories ten years prior with the entire family, my understanding wife only slightly reluctantly agreed not to spend our twenty-fifth in Mexico but rather in Colorado. Since that original family vacation I have built a small barn with three stalls and a nice fenced-in pasture and ultimately purchased or bred seven enjoyable horses.

As a direct result of getting thrown off of Sydney, one of our original two horses, when she was a two-year-old and breaking my left wrist and right elbow, I pursued a greater knowledge of the psychological makeup of my beloved horse. To accomplish this goal I decided to learn from the best horse trainer family in the world, John and Josh Lyons from Parachute, Colorado.

Completing the Lyons school was both a physical and emotional test of fortitude. Perhaps the Lyons school was a precursor to other physical and emotional challenges to come just a few years later.

Lucky, unlucky day of my life

The 2008 school year started out like most every year. Most years start out a little difficult and then improve as the students' motivation. As a teacher at East High School, like most teachers all over America, the idea of closing in on the fourth quarter and the end of the school year is truly something we all look forward to.

Let me preface everything by stating in advance that about twenty-five years ago my doctor determined that I had high cholesterol. Since then I had been taking medication daily to control my bad cholesterol (low-density lipoproteins [LDL]). I had also started taking one aspirin daily due to the many TV news recommendations. While I accepted with apprehension the doctor telling me twenty-five years ago that high cholesterol could bring heart disease that was still the furthest thought from my mind at the time. I was not overweight; my diet was well balanced except for an occasional Tombstone Pizza, much to my wife's dismay. I had no family history of heart problems, no diabetes in the family, never smoked, and only practiced extremely mild drinking, maybe a couple per week (thank you, Coors Beer).

The exercise routine I followed since 2004 could be described as a weekend cowboy athletic program. In 2004 I attended and graduated from the John and Josh Lyons Certified Horse Training Program (www.johnlyons.com) in Parachute, Colorado.

As an educator I constantly search potentially groundbreaking new methods of becoming a more effective teacher. As a horse lover I also looked for a method contrary to the "cowboy" methods of teaching a horse. Given the fact that thankfully corporal punishment has been essentially eradicated as a manner of motivating students to perform to

Standing proud with Josh Lyons at graduation

their optimum level, I hoped that somehow the old method of beating a horse to learn or respond could also be nullified as a less-intelligent and less-effective horse-training method. Not only did the Lyons' training prove that beating a horse is not necessary, but it also provided thoughts about listening to students in the classroom environment.

Teaching children to accomplish certain objectives or pass certain tests, I discovered, can be mirrored with the art of teaching horses. While attending John Lyons' certified horse training program I found that "the conditional response" method of teaching a horse provided for exceptional outcomes in horse training.

The classroom for a horse is the horse trainers' classroom, called a round pen, often sixty feet in diameter. Effective training of a horse requires a great deal of movement, and physical fitness is critical on the part of the horse trainer.

Working with student in the conventional classroom also takes a great deal of walking and sometimes running to be effective. Between training clients' horses on the weekends and sometimes during the weeknights and actively teaching during the week, my cardiovascular workouts I thought were sufficient.

Until March 31, 2008, I considered myself to be in pretty good physical shape as a result of an active lifestyle spent training horses but also actively teaching in the classroom. To say I was content and happy with my life would be a huge understatement.

On the morning of March 31 I arrived at school at about 7:50 AM to finish third-quarter grades and begin planning for what I hoped would be an exciting and rewarding fourth quarter (perhaps a little exaggerated). Around 8:00 AM the very tips of both shoulder blades started to become uncomfortable, much like the feeling of a pulled or sore muscle. As I continued to input the third-quarter grades I decided that the discomfort was growing and should be addressed by visiting the school nurse for a couple of Advil.

As a responsible school nurse, Robin asked me the typical questions such as what might be causing the discomfort. My response was my happy-go-lucky explanation that those who know me have come to expect, that I had thrown hay on Saturday for the horses (unloading 150 fifty-pound bales into the horse barn from a large hay rack), and used a chain saw all day Sunday to cut down dead trees and limbs around the house to be used in our fireplace and in our outdoor fire pit for bonfires.

For the next thirty-five minutes while I arduously completed the third-quarter grades, the Advil provided by Robin seemed to have accomplished their goal. Unfortunately, the pain started to reappear in the same location on the tips of both shoulder blades thirty minutes later, this time with greater intensity.

Once I completed the grading I walked down the hallway and stairs toward the first-floor office to submit my third-quarter grades. At the time, I mentioned to the office staff that my shoulder blades were sore due to throwing hay and chain-sawing down trees. We all laughed and commented on how physically strenuous weekends can be as we grow older. One of the office staff, Vicki, who happened to be a high school friend and never one to miss an opportunity for a dig, made mention that the soreness had more to do with old age. Never one to avoid an opportunity myself, I did not fail to remind her that she was twenty-five days older than me. While the fun and laughter in the office did redirect thoughts of my shoulder blades' discomfort, it really did not dissipate, and it just more or less lingered.

After leaving the office I spent time chatting and joking with students already in the hallway like I did on most days. The pain I was experiencing in my shoulder blades slowly increased, but no more than what I expected to be present from throwing hay and cutting trees.

At 8:40 the shoulder blade pain started to intensify yet again. Unlike the breaking of an arm and a wrist, where the pain after breaking a bone decreases pretty quickly after the break and almost becomes a dull pain, this pain had no mercy or sign of diminishing. The best way I can describe it was as if someone were tightening wood screws into my shoulder blades.

Not having a clue what was happening I started to do a variety of (in hindsight) really stupid things to try to make the pain go away. I started to do shoulder rolls, baseball pitching windmills, shoulder stretches against my chest, and even a few jumping jacks to relieve what I thought was shoulder soreness from weekend work.

At about 9:00 AM one of the school's assistant principals, Deena Hunter-Lantz, happened to walk into my classroom. Deena visiting my classroom was not a normal event in either of our daily routines. Deena and I have had a great relationship over the years and we were often joking. On this day she noticed that something was wrong with me right away. She quickly noticed me doing my (ill-advised) exercises, and I made the sarcastic comment that she should stop tightening down the wood screws in my shoulders because I had just handed in my third-quarter grades (normally she was in charge of teachers handing in grade sheets). The more the two of us joked, the more the pain seemed to intensify.

After what seemed like hours but was actually only twenty minutes or so, the pain became unbearably excruciating to say the least. At no time did I have any consideration that I was having anything more than very painful shoulder pain related to throwing hay and chain-sawing down trees, as the pain remained 100 percent on the tip of both shoulder blades.

I never experienced any shortness of breath, chest pains, arm numbness, or anything else that might have had me suspect anything besides some muscular pain.

At approximately 9:10, Deena and I made the decision that Robin, the school nurse, should be called for some assistance. Robin arrived shortly and again immediately asked me the obvious questions about what hurt and why it could be causing such pain. Keeping with typical sarcasm, I once again blamed Deena for the pain and her tightening of the wood screws further and further, tighter and tighter into my shoulder blades. It was at this point that my level of anxiety began to grow as the pain never seemed to decrease but rather increased.

Pretty quickly we all agreed that an ambulance should be called as the pain was reaching the point where I was nearly crying from its immensity. Around 9:15 the ambulance arrived at the rear entrance of the school. In the meantime the pain had become out of this world. On a pain scale of one to ten, I would classify it somewhere in the ballpark of a 1,312, and that may even be an understatement. Within just a few minutes the paramedics arrived in my classroom and immediately asked me the same redundant questions related to what was hurting and why as I blamed Deena yet again. (I hope everyone at this point realizes that I like to joke with people, and laughing, I thought, was a way to mitigate the pain.)

Within perhaps two minutes I was placed on the gurney, rushed down the hallway to the elevator, and taken down to the ground level to access the ambulance. As the paramedics wheeled me into the ambulance they asked for my preferred hospital, which is common practice. I conveyed the insurance company's preferred hospital, but before I even finished they interrupted my response. They immediately conveyed, "We don't think so; you're going to Swedes (Swedish American Hospital http://www.swedishamerican.org)." Looking back I remember being pretty confused as to why they said that. I remember asking myself why St. Anthony Hospital (http://www. osfsaintanthony.org) was not close enough. The travel time from East to St. Anthony with traffic that time of day would have been ten to fifteen minutes. On the other hand the travel time for Swedish American was less than three minutes. I thought to myself what the heck was that time sensitive with muscle problems or a bad back.

The first thing that ran through my mind was the insurance nightmare that was going to take place because these guys, the EMT personnel, refused to take me to the other hospital for a back problem as I still did not sense the true emergency.

I had no idea why the EMTs refused to go to the preferred hospital. I had no idea at the time that the travel time to my insurance company's preferred hospital would have been greater than the five-minute window allocated to the "widow maker" heart attack and that going to that hospital would have resulted in my death.

Shortly after I was placed in the ambulance the EMT handed me four baby aspirin and said that I should take them very quickly. In my mind I had no idea what was causing the extreme pain in my shoulders, but what I did realize immediately was that four baby aspirin would not eliminate the intense pain. My mind immediately started flashing back to the articles I had read and the news stories I had watched about ambulances and children's aspirin. While my mind raced to remember the articles and newscasts regarding the administering of baby aspirin, I kept on telling myself that it was not me that these stories focused on as I was having shoulder blade pain. At that point the EMTs asked if they could contact my wife. I reached for my cell phone while lying on the gurney and handed it to them, telling them how to find my contact list and make the phone call. Within about ten seconds of taking the children's aspirin and handing the EMTs my cell phone, I died the first time.

"You need to stay focused"

Chapter 3

I remember the bounce of lowering my gurney onto the hard ground as we arrived to the hospital. At this point I continued to be clueless as to what was really going on. I had no idea that I had "coded" (I have learned a few new terms, like "coded" versus dead). I remember thinking that if my gurney had wings I would have been flying as they ran me into the emergency room for attention. I remember asking myself if my wife was actually going to come to the hospital, as I had told Deena to tell my wife as it was only a back problem.

I remember watching people rushing around the emergency room working with a great deal of urgency. I remember asking myself if back pain could be so serious that such urgency would be required in an emergency room. Again the doctors and nurses asked me the same rather redundant questions that I had been asked earlier by school staff and paramedics. This time, however, the questions were more in depth, and there were more of them. It was then for the first time that I sensed a level of deeper concern. To this day I remember looking into the eyes of the doctors asking me the questions and trying to read their minds regarding what was going on. The one feeling I did get was that this moment was not a "*Mr. Rogers' Neighborhood*" event. (I know that is a rather corny thought, but at the time I really had no idea what to think other than being a little corny.)

I did not exactly know what they were getting at when they asked the questions, and upon reflection maybe I did not want to know, but I honestly still had no idea what was going on other than my back shoulder blade pain still existed.

Do I have high blood pressure? Do I smoke? Do I drink (excessively, I think)? Do I have high cholesterol? Did anyone in my family have heart problems? Have I had shortness of breath? To all the questions I responded no with exception of cholesterol and shortness of breath. I told them that I had been taking medicine for twenty-five-plus years for the cholesterol and wouldn't you be short of breath over the weekend if you had been throwing hay for horses and chain-sawing down trees? The doctors and nurses responded with a nod and a laugh.

Perhaps this is when I went into the denial mode. I processed that I was not having anything but back problems given the fact that I completely passed the heart disease barrage of questions. I remember looking around the emergency room trying to listen to the doctors and nurses and attempting to figure out what was going on that caused everyone to work quickly and talk with a rather urgent tone of voice. Then, as if I were falling asleep without the feeling of fatigue, shortly after finishing the barrage of questions, unbeknownst to me I died, or "coded," for the second time.

As if awakening from a nap with my wife softly touching my cheeks, when I awoke this time a nurse was doing just that while I lay in the emergency room. I remember like it happened yesterday the nurse softly touching my cheeks and telling me that "you need to focus." I must have looked at her with a totally confused manner as she then went on to explain that "you keep on leaving us. You're a very, very lucky individual that the paramedics got you here in three minutes and twenty seconds. Anything more than five minutes would have been too long. If you leave us again, we will have to run you up to the cath lab (cardiac catheter lab)."

Looking back, this is where I should have asked the most obvious question of the day—"What the heck is going on?" Perhaps, I guess, I really did not want to know the answer as the entire event was so far outside anything I had ever experienced.

It was then as I lay in the emergency room, and not until then, that I had any idea how serious the situation really was. While before I watched the doctors and nurses scurrying around the emergency room frantically doing their jobs, I found myself transfixing my eyes on the ceiling of the emergency room. My mind suddenly did what is portrayed on the TV and movies, as it went into the Hollywood mode of thinking about everything done or undone in my life.

I thought about how I was far too young to leave my kids without a father. I thought about my daughter, Stephanie, who was twenty-three at the time. I thought about not being able to walk her down the wedding aisle someday when she gets married, and how difficult it would be for her to do it without me. I thought about my son, Brandon, who was living so far away, now working on a career with Disney World and alone, and how I could no longer be there to offer advice. I thought about how my children would handle not getting their ritual text message every morning when I wake up saying, "Good morning … love ya … have a great day."

I thought about my wife and all she has done putting up with me for almost twenty-six married years plus five years prior, as we were the product of a high school romance. What hit me like a ton of bricks were the thoughts of how bad I would feel if I left her with many things she would no longer need or want and would become an unwanted burden very quickly.

I continued to think about the log home of our dreams that had stretched our finances, the six horses that we owned and seemed very important just hours earlier, the dream Dodge Laramie 3500, dually, heavy-duty, 4x4 truck that I had dreamt about for years and finally acquired, and finally the dream of owning a three-horse slant Featherlite horse trailer that we had bought the previous September. All of these material objects that seemed so very critical to a happy life on March 30 suddenly became a burden that I would hate myself for leaving my wife with if I were not to make it. I started to shed my first tears, not because of the pain but because I had so many things left undone or unfinished.

Looking back I remember thinking how bad I felt that my wife would be coming to the hospital. This was the final week of rehearsals for the spring musical that she was directing, and I knew how much effort she and the students put into the yearly musical. As I lay in the bed I just had the feeling that Jennifer was on her way from Dakota High School (http://www.dakota201.com) where she teaches. I remember so badly wanting to tell her to go back to school and don't miss rehearsal as I was going to be fine … it was nothing.

As I lay in the emergency room for what seemed like forever but I am sure was only a minute or perhaps seconds, I started thinking about my brothers, sisters, and parents. I thought about hurt feelings between siblings, time not spent with them due to growing my own family and time constraints that started to dominate my life. I made promises to myself, if I made it, related to matters of family.

Suddenly, I imagined the conversation that my wife might be having at the same moment with my children and family telling them about my situation. I started to cry again. My heart sank, literally and figuratively. The next thing I realized was that I was flying, yet again, on a gurney down the hallway as I must have not kept focused as told to avoid the dying or that now dreaded "coding" thing again that the nurse had warned me earlier. I realize now that I had just experienced death number three. The path between the emergency room and cath lab seemed to take a quite a while. I just remember holding onto the side of the gurney.

I am not sure exactly when, but while flying down the hallway en route to the cath lab, I realized that all my pain had gone away. I realize now that the only thing I was feeling was that I was very, very scared. My eyes must have looked as big as saucers in the cath lab as I remember looking around the room. I remember all the TV screens showing black-and-white images. I vaguely remember the nurses looking for and finding places to insert IVs or other objects.

I remember the tone of some statements between nurses and doctors as being nervous or cautiously optimistic. I remember clearly my thoughts hanging heavily on the "nervous or cautious" tones of a couple statements regarding the need to "stabilize him."

I clearly remember the soft touch of the doctors and nurses. And yet at the same time, I no longer felt in any way the extreme pain that I had been feeling just a few minutes before in the emergency room and ambulance. As with before, I felt as though I fell asleep yet again. Later, I was told that I had coded for the fourth and fifth times (at this time the word died is becoming too difficult to type, let alone think).

I remember these feelings as if they happened just a few moments ago. I felt desperately alone at the time, wanting so badly to have someone next to me whom I was familiar with holding my hand. I so badly wanted to feel the touch of my wife, son, or daughter in the crook of my shoulder. I just wanted this stark, cold-looking room to go away. I just wanted to see a loved one in the next two seconds, as I felt very alone. It was then that I felt a tear cascade down my right cheek. Then without warning I fell "asleep" (easier than saying coding or dying at this point) for the sixth time. This time shocking me back required one shock at normal setting and a second one at full power.

Very bright light

I am not quite sure when the bright light appeared, but I can't help but think it was the last time I coded. I guess when you pound on heaven's door as many times as I did, somebody will eventually answer the door. In reflection, I vividly remember the very bright light and that it had no discernable shapes or figures as part of it. I remember feeling that I was completely awake in a tunnel and literally standing and looking toward the bright light. I clearly remember pausing and debating to myself that I was completely aware and cognizant in every manner that I enjoy on a daily basis.

For some reason I don't know if I will ever understand or realize I never chose to walk toward the bright light. I just stood there in the tunnel, which was rather large in diameter. What I do remember is that I felt at complete ease with the situation, and a wash of calm came over me about everything. Without warning the tunnel that I was standing in suddenly went dark. I know that is rather vague at best, but that is the best I can do to recall the moment.

It was in the cath lab that I had angioplasty performed on me.

Angioplasty as I know now is where a balloon-like catheter is snaked to where the blockage in the artery is found. The balloon is then inflated to push the blockage to the outer wall of the artery. This is followed by another catheter that puts the stent into place. I was told later that I had a 100 percent blocked left anterior descending artery that brought on my heart attack. Without the insertion of the heart stent I would not be alive today.

When the cath lab scene came into vision I felt a rush of calm and confidence. I guessed that I had made it. The TV screens became interesting, and the talk tone changed to more optimistic; that was a much better feeling. It was then that all my previous thoughts about family, siblings, and material objects started to clear up and I realized that I had another chance. More importantly, I for some strange reason lost the "scared out of my wits" feeling that I had previously felt.

The next thing I remember hearing was that they needed to "put in a catheter." The idea of someone inserting a flexible tube into the end of my genitalia in order to pass urine is something that is a very uncomfortable thought or action.

I realized for the first time that indeed I had some feeling in my body; definitely not the way I would have liked to find out. It was three years prior that I had the forgettable opportunity to experience yet another wide-awake catheter installation. The previous experience was completely unrelated to this event. The only similarity was that it too was completely unexpected, with no risk factors. That time it was being experienced prior to a horrible bout of diverticulitis that required colon surgery.

As I lay there trying to forget the uncomfortable feeling of insertion of the catheter, I found my mind wondering how bad it was, and if there would be any long-lasting side-effects or massive problems that would be a large burden for all my loved ones. I could feel nothing related to my body, which really concerned me at the time.

The next thing I remember was awakening for the first time in a room other than an emergency room or cath lab. I was almost relieved to see the walls of an ICU (intensive care unit) room. As I woke up I struggled to understand what I had just gone through. I had no idea what to expect as I started to gather my senses. I wondered in a fast-forward manner if I had any damages that might affect speech or movement to any degree. When I was initially unable to speak, my mind raced and thought the worst thoughts possible. I was literally scared to death (no pun intended) that I was going to be in a vegetable state for the rest of my life.

I am sure that during my brief visit in the ambulance, emergency room, and the cath lab I was indeed having a heart attack, but to this day I could take a lie detector test and pass with flying colors if asked if at any time I became aware that I was suffering a heart attack. My answer to that question would be one word: NO.

I remember thinking that I was completely aware of everything but did not have the ability to move or feel my arms, legs, or any other part of my body. The more moments that passed without the return of the bodily senses, such as feeling my body and moving my arms and legs, the more frightened I became. I felt like a newborn baby unable to speak or function.

The more I felt that I would be forever kept alive as a vegetable, the more my emotions became exaggerated, and I am sure my blood pressure escalated. I so badly wanted to talk to my wife, daughter, and son and hold them tight as I have never done before; I was an emotional mess.

In addition to the horrific feeling of being a vegetable, I was panicked that I also could not speak. All I realized was that I could not talk. I failed to rationalize that I could not speak because I had a ventilator or ET tube (endotracheal tube) down my esophagus. The more seconds that passed while not having any feeling, not being able to move or speak, the more I realized I was nearing the panic state of mind. It seemed like several minutes—but my timeline is, I am sure, distorted—until the feelings of my arms, legs, and body returned. As the feeling in my extremities came back I remember a deep sense of relief.

My inability to express myself was scaring the hell out of me. I wanted nothing more than to tell my family how much I loved them and not to worry. I wanted to express to them how horrible I felt that I had put them through such a horrible experience. Regretfully, with great frustration, I realized that a breathing tube was down my throat, preventing me from having any of these needed conversations.

Shortly after getting many of my feelings back while lying in the ICU I realized very quickly that the upper area of my chest really hurt. I had no idea why, but one thing for sure was that it hurt. The more my senses came back, the more often I found myself thanking God for not making me a vegetable. I started to realize what I could and could not do. I badly wanted to take a deep breath. I had often told my students at school when they were dealing with a problem in their life to "Take a deep breath … and get over it." Once again my mind started to race. I guess that I started to think perhaps the worst had happened. I had no idea what the "worst" could be, but I knew that what I was experiencing was way outside any reality that I had ever faced before in my life.

The more time passed (probably a matter of just a few minutes, if that), the more exasperated I became with what I thought was the slow passing of time. I was all hooked up to stuff and I had no idea why it was attached to me. While I know saying this is rather redundant, my repeated feeling of wanting desperately to hold my wife, daughter, and son in my arms as tight as I could kept returning. I was totally and utterly frustrated by the situation. I felt that I was sharp mentally and that physically I was really in a bad place, and worst of all I could not hug and talk to those I so deeply love. I hated that feeling more than anything I had experienced before.

As reality started to set in, and thankfully not a moment too soon, my wife appeared in my room. I felt a great sense of relief, but the frustration of not being able to hold her with all of the strength in my arms was an agony that I would never wish on anyone else.

I tried with all my ability to relax and breathe softly, but the discomfort I felt in my body was beginning to become more of an issue. It was not really excruciating pain like what I had just an hour earlier but more of a disconcerting inability to breathe naturally. The more I tried to focus on relaxing as my wife, nurses, and doctors coached me to do, the more the things seemed to go physically in the wrong direction. Everything physically related to my body became quickly more uncomfortable and alarming.

It was at this point that I found myself starting to get really ticked off at the situation. I just did not understand the answer to that question "Why me?" Three years prior when I had a really bad bout with diverticulitis, my incredible doctor and friend, Larry, came to the conclusion that I had no risk factors associated with the diverticulitis problem at the time it occurred.

After two rather involved surgeries with the colon problem and a change of lifestyle as a result, I found myself asking myself how I could be the chosen one to have something this bad happening.

It was at this moment when my mind went from bad to worse after the "Why me?" thoughts related to another emergency medical situation started to really consume my line of thought and I am sure did not help my already anxious and frustrated disposition.

I CAN'T BREATHE

The more time I spent awake, the more worried I became about my physical well-being. I could not communicate verbally to discover why I was hooked up to all of the machines. I began discovering how quickly life changes. I thought to myself that I am forty-eight years old, healthy, active, with a great diet—this entire experience does not add up.

I felt totally confused and helpless, especially since I could not ask how bad the situation really was, which only compounded the overwhelming emotions. My heart and emotions started to flounder like a struggling horse stuck in mud. My life was completely out of my control, which is a terrible feeling. I so badly wanted to get up, get dressed, and get the heck out of the hospital. I felt like someone had pushed the fast-forward button on my life and it was racing out of my control. Worst of all, I could not verbally communicate to my family that mentally I was okay and lucid and what the hell was going on? I wanted my wife to know that I was still there mentally but could only communicate with my eyes.

As much as I tried to communicate with my eyes, I failed in a big way. As the frustration rose to very scary heights, I felt a physical frustration that I have never in my forty-eight years of life felt before. As the frustration mounted, as I am sure my blood pressure did as well, my physical body started to do uncontrollably scary things. As my feeling continued to return more and more, I realized that my breathing was not as fluid as I had for so long taken for granted. I had taken everything for granted physically up until then. I felt a haunting feeling that I was unable to breathe. I could not take that cleansing deep breath that had become a part of my daily ritual for calming down.

I was able to motion enough to my wife and nurses that I wanted to write down feelings and needs on a piece of paper. I found myself laughing internally when all they could find for my writing was a small almost Post-it note size tablet. However, my wife claims that it was a full size pad of paper. While it may not have been noticeable to anyone else, I wanted to ask out loud with a great deal of sarcasm, "Do you think you could find anything else smaller for me to write on?"

The anxiety of not being able to speak when waking up and becoming cognizant of surroundings is incredibly scary. In my opinion hospitals should make available to each patient a method of communication by actually handing them a pad of paper and a pencil. The more I struggled to communicate that I wanted a pencil and paper to communicate, the more I became frustrated and angry. Not a good thing, given the situation.

I found myself struggling more mentally about how I could convey my feelings or questions on a note pad. The more I found myself wanting to communicate and grasping the reality that I could not, even with the assistance of a note pad, the more the frustration was beginning to consume me physically and emotionally.

It was then for the first time out of the wild-blue yonder that I inexplicably and with no warning of the slightest nature vomited for the first time. I vividly remember looking at my wife first and then at the nurses who were tending to my medical needs. My emotions took a very abrupt turn south and my emotions hit new lows. It was at this point that everything seemed to go into slow motion. If my eyes could scream my scared feelings, Chicago (ninety miles southeast of Rockford) would have heard my "Oh my God; this is bad" statement that my eyes screamed.

I suddenly felt every bad thought that I probably could have thought at the time. I was struggling to breath, the discomfort in my chest was mounting, sensors were hooked up everywhere, and tubes seemed to be stuck in my arms more than ever before in my life—and now the ultimate icing on a dreadful cake. I was vomiting uncontrollably without warning and could not function normally. I found myself looking at everything the doctors had attached to my body, and I lost it emotionally and wanted to rip out every medical device attached to me. I wanted life to return to where it was earlier in the day. I wanted to teach like I do every day. This really sucked.

Suddenly, the idea of not breathing and dying started to race into my thoughts. As I looked into my wife's eyes I could see frustration, deep concern, and worry. I know that she was trying with everything within her ability to calm me, but after thirty-two years together, emotions and eye language speak much louder than any spoken word. The frustration I felt was only compounded by the raging level of embarrassment of yakking in front of other people that I did not know. Yakking is something that should take place in the privacy of the bathroom with no other person around. As the nurses tending to me removed my hospital gown, the feeling of embarrassment washed over me yet again. I did not want anyone to see me lying there with vomit all over me and someone washing my naked body. I badly wanted to cover up. I know that those feelings are more than slightly silly given the situation, but nonetheless they were very real.

It was about then that my daughter, Stephanie, and son, Brandon, walked into the room. I desperately wanted to hold them tight in my arms and tell them that I was okay. I so badly wanted to reach out and pull both of them to me for a big hug or at least to hold them tight in my arms. As my daughter came into my sight she responded more to what she saw than to what I needed at the time. My son just looked the tough guy role. As I looked into my daughter's eyes I saw a young woman who was looking like she was in shock and that something was very, very, very wrong with her father. At the sight of her face and eyes I could only imagine how she must have handled the phone call from her mother. I could not imagine how long the drive she and her boyfriend, J, had from Chicago. It must have been the longest hour and half that she had ever experienced.

I instantaneously felt like a real schmuck for putting her in this very bad situation. I could see in her eyes, much like her mother's, the worry and helpless feeling of the moment. I physically wanted badly to get out of bed, walk over to her, and hold her like I had so often done when she was young and as she grew up to be a very special young lady. She walked in and seemed to find a place as far away from my bed as she could. I am sure that it was not actually the case, but it seemed like it in my state of mind. I wanted her to get into my bed and put her head on my shoulder as she had hundreds of times before as she grew up. The frustration of the moment and seeing her eyes of worry and concern gave me an even greater sense that things were not going in the right direction.

It was then, to the best of my recollection, that I threw up or aspirated for the second time. I realized that I was totally coming unglued emotionally. My emotional frustrations were hitting uncharted levels. I was hooked up to lots of things, I was already struggling with the breathing program, and my chest was feeling rather uncomfortable.

I had already once been totally embarrassed from the original aspiration, and now with my daughter and my wife standing nearby I uncontrollably threw up for the third time. With that, my daughter jumped back and ran out of the room. I was devastated, and my level of being scared went much higher as I saw her run out of room.

As I lay there with black vomit all over me, I kept praying that the nurses would not take off my gown yet again and start washing off my body in case my daughter decided to enter the room again. I realized that I was getting tense and anxious wanting to get a towel to cover up very quickly before she walked back into my room.

It was then that it seemed to me that everything seemed to go from bad to worse emotionally for me regarding worry about loved ones. Those around me were seeing their dad and husband do things that I would never want them to see, given the choice.

It was then that breathing became difficult at best, or to put a finer point on it "damn difficult." I began to feel as though I was starting to suffocate or drown right in front of my loved ones' concerned and worried eyes and that I had no control over the situation. I looked into the eyes of my wife and for the first time since leaving the cath lab I realized that maybe I was not going to make it and I just wanted to scream to her how much I loved her as I struggled to breathe.

It was then that I heard the statement from the medical staff that I needed an NG (nasal gastric) tube up my nasal passage. For anyone who is wondering about the feelings related to the insertion of an NG tube, let me say it in laymen's terms: it hurt like a son of a bitch! The pain level for insertion of that godforsaken tube went way past the one-to-ten scale of pain. To put it in perspective, I would rather have a catheter inserted and extracted from my genitalia five times than to ever have an NG tube inserted once while I remained awake.

I thought for sure that I was on death's doorstep. The eye language of my wife and daughter, as much as they tried to put on a happy face, failed to eradicate the doorstep thought. My breathing became more difficult before it got any better from the insertion of the NG tube. I am sure that it helped in reality; but in my reality, it did nothing but make me feel like I was suffocating in a slightly slower death.

Why do I feel like crap?

Chapter 6

As I continued to struggle with the NG tube all I could hear from the medical staff was that I needed to relax. I remember thinking slightly sarcastically once again, "You all must be joking," or with the same sarcastic-laced thought, "Does anyone have a sense of reality at all? This situation really sucks." I remember thinking to myself that things were probably not as bad as I thought they were, but given the last few hours of experiences, my mind was not in the most rational state.

As I lay there with the breathing tube down my throat and the NG tube painfully up my nose and feeling the discomfort of my chest, I started to run the same two questions through my mind over and over again: "What did I do to deserve this?" combined almost simultaneously with the equally troublesome question "Why me?" I knew at the time that my thoughts were not exactly the most Christian of thoughts, but I found myself thinking of all those people in the world who were in poor health, fat or even obese, heavy smokers, walked around with a negative attitude, ate fried food on a daily basis, consumed bacon like I used to eat Chuckles candy, and those people who did not generally care about their health.

I could mentally process about anything I wanted to consider. I remember doing mental calisthenics in an effort to prove to myself that I was capable and sharp and that more than anything perhaps everything was not that bad. I started to consider what possibly my substitute teacher in my classroom could be teaching today and how the students were handling the vision of a teacher getting wheeled into the ambulance in front of them. I even thought about the question of who would step up and feed and water the horses at home. Finally, I questioned to myself how my wife was going to finish rehearsals for the spring musical, *Pippin,* that she was putting on at Dakota High School where she taught.

The more I contemplated these questions, the more I was able to convince myself that I had my mental ability to reason. I, however, lacked the comfort of knowing that I could actually communicate verbally due to the breathing tube down my throat. I envisioned myself with thoughts caught inside me and physical damage that would not allow me to speak again. I was very scared and petrified at the prospect of living with the disability of not being able to communicate with my loved ones as I have done for so long.

The more time my mind had to dwell on the worst thoughts possible, the more anxious, nervous, and upset I became. The feeling of suffocating was not improving by leaps and bounds, and the anxiety of dying seemed to show up from time to time. My desire to take a large deep breath was huge. On the contrary, I had to focus on total relaxation and soft, shallow breathing. That goal was much more difficult than I could have ever thought possible.

As much as I tried to stay alert and awake, I remember zoning in and out of zombie land. One minute I was pretty sure I was coherent, thinking about tomorrow and what I would have the substitute teacher assign to the students in my absence, and the next moment everything was fuzzy; although I tried to keep listening to everyone, the words became at best foggy and incomprehensible. I badly wanted to attempt to speak to my wife, my daughter, my son, and her boyfriend, J, when they arrived. The desire was there, but the ability was frustratingly not. I am sure at the time I comprehended part of what they were all saying, so it is a good thing that they tried. What I so badly wanted was for my daughter to sit on one side of the bed and my wife on the other and just hold my hand and squeeze so I could feel the feeling of the squeeze.

The more I tried to relax and breathe, the more I started to understand and cherish the thought that I had made it and that whatever happened to me, I could survive. I started to contemplate the here and now. What exactly was going on right now? How did I end up being brought here? Finally, how was I going to fix this crappy situation? I started to scan the room, looking at all that they had attached to me. I wondered why each was attached and what the heck they were doing.

The more those questions went through my mind, the more I realized that I was getting overly frustrated because I could not answer the questions. It was at that point that I decided to focus on family and loved ones. I started to think about vacations, my hopes of moving to Colorado, extended family matters, horses and how much fun they are, and more important than anything else, how the heck I was going to get out of this situation and hospital.

Regardless of the diligence I was putting toward thinking about other things that would minimize the situation at hand, the reality was that my chest really hurt. I felt like I had just competed in the Olympic decathlon. I felt exhausted and fatigued. My arms and legs felt like they each weighed at least five hundred pounds. I know the thought is kind of funny now, but even my head felt like at least two hundred pounds. There was not one body part that I felt motivated to voluntarily move.

The one peculiar thing about everything to this point related to the ICU was that I remember very little of what was said by anyone. Just about the only thing I remember was when the nurses were trying to get me to calm down and breathe easier so as not to vomit again. I am sure my wife spoke and that my children were saying a great deal to me, but I had a great deal of difficulty dealing with anything other than the total shock of what had happened. The more I contemplated the entire situation, the more I was totally being consumed by fear and nervousness, but I found it completely impossible not to be.

The more I became aware of my surroundings and the situation at hand, the more I started to get very apprehensive about the idea of sleeping that evening. I was completely aware of the fact that it was still early in the day and bedtime was a good distance way, but I became more and more nervous every time I found myself fading into darkness and then to light again. I realized that I had made it by this point and pretty much summed up the really crappy situation I was in. The next moment in a rather lucid thought I would immediately think about bedtime when life would go dark again. I remember vividly that there was a moment when my loved ones were preoccupied and without warning I once again shed a couple tears brought on by being scared to sleep later in the day.

I would suggest very strongly that any hospital provide for a waiver of the rule that no visitors are permitted to sleep overnight the first two nights. I would urge all hospitals to make available a comfortable La-Z-Boy-like chair that could be placed close enough to the patient to hold hands with the patient until a comfortable level of sleep was established. If I had known that the hospital had a policy that encouraged loved ones to be close by during the first two nights I would have had less anxiety prior to going to bed. I caught myself more that several times looking for a clock, anticipating the moment when it was time to actually go to bed.

By mid-afternoon that first day my faculties started to return ever so slowly, it seemed. I tried with all my being to listen to conversations, but all I could understand was jabber. Everything that was being told to me seemed to be told to me through the blades a running fan. I just did not get it no matter how hard I tried.

For the previous several years I had made it a habit when stressed or experiencing a tough moment in my life when I needed to relax to take a deep breath and exhale it slowly. For the last several hours I found myself unable to even come close to taking that relaxing deep breath. It hurt. With each breath I attempted to take, it constantly felt like my older brother John was sitting on my chest holding me down when we were much younger and wrestling. The only difference I was having that day was that in addition to the feeling of John sitting on my chest there was also the feeling that someone had first beat on my chest like a drum and bruised every inch of it (no, John never did that). It's not that I could not breathe, but they had to be shallow breaths at best in order not to cause a substantially uncomfortable discomfort on my chest.

Family members. But why?

Chapter 7

There came a point in the afternoon when my wife told me that my family was there waiting to see me. I am not sure if I asked by writing on a note pad, or perhaps I asked it to myself, but I wondered how bad things were. I was pretty much in a state of denial about practically everything. At the time she told me about my family, I honestly had no idea why my parents, brothers, and sisters would be at the hospital.

I was only beginning to put my arms around the idea that I had a little scare of a heart attack. At that point I remember telling myself that I will be out of here soon and back to school by the end of the week. After all … it was not that bad. So why was everyone there? It was not until my wife made mention that even Sue, my sister, was there that I even gave a thought to how bad it really was. To this day I remember the sinking feeling when I was told that Sue was also at the hospital. I was completely aware of the fact that she had driven all the way from Rib Mountain, Wisconsin, on a Monday and how many hours there are between Rockford and Rib Mountain. My heart sank again, and emotionally I got a little depressed at what might be going on.

I felt horrible that my family was going to see me with the NG tube and the breathing tube in place. I felt rather helpless and

Family and loved ones in hospital waiting room

embarrassed at the thought of them seeing me in that situation. I so badly wanted to actually talk to everyone who came to visit. It was very emotionally frustrating seeing my parents and brothers and sisters without having the ability to speak.

I remember checking the time of day and wondering what the heck everyone was doing there at that time of day. What did they know that I did not? As each and every brother and sister took their turn after my parents, I felt more and more confused with the situation. I remember thinking to myself at the time that it seemed like an episode of *The Twilight Zone* when everything seems to be surreal but real at the same time. I was definitely missing the boat when it came to understanding the true situation of the moment.

With each loved one came a look in their eyes of being very scared for the moment. Small talk was attempted on each of their parts, but their eyes spoke volumes related to their feelings. I could see that they were trying to say the right things about the situation at hand, but they were as much in shock as I was at that moment.

Shortly after realizing that the situation might be worse than I thought and that is why all my family was at the hospital came the appreciation that each and every one of my siblings and my parents were there. That seemed to uplift my feelings.

As much as I truly enjoyed and absorbed good feelings from loved ones and siblings, my very astute wife could see how quickly I was beginning to look exhausted that first day. She made the difficult decision to start limiting well-wishers from my room for the next couple of days. At the time I thought she was wrong, but shortly thereafter I realized that her heart was in the right place and that limiting visitors on the first day was indeed a brilliant idea, as I found myself mentally and physically exhausted.

With the feeling of exhaustion came the feeling of being scared, as I realized that the day would be ending soon and sleep would be soon after. With every tick of the clock, I realized that I did not want to fall asleep and let my life go dark again. I started to really hate the idea of going to sleep. I was scared to death that I would not wake up in the morning. I started to really need my wife, daughter, and son as close as I could get them to me, but I still could not communicate because of the NG and breathing tube.

I understood completely by late afternoon that I was not destined to be a human vegetable for the rest of my life, but the frustration of not being able to speak, just lying there with a tube up my nose and another down my throat was beginning to drive me crazy. I wanted to talk and understand everything going on with me. I tried with every molecule of my being to listen and understand everything that was being said to me or about me. I am sure that if they had a monitor that detected anxiety and frustration hooked to me with everything else it would have been off the charts. I vividly remember my overwhelming desire to rip off everything attached to me, stand up, and get a huge family hug.

As much as I felt guilty about screwing up my wife's high school musical rehearsals, I did not want her to leave the room until I left the room myself. I have always been someone people described as having a positive attitude about life. I frequently made the statement that the cup is half full versus half empty. In this instance, I had grave concerns that I would not wake the next morning. There was a point when my mind daydreamed to loved ones walking by my coffin and crying. My heart literally dropped a foot and I shed one very large tear with that thought. At the time my wife was talking to doctors and I quickly wiped my tear away.

Late in the afternoon was very much the lowest point for me psychologically between 9:30 AM on that first day until now, my one-year anniversary. The conversation I heard that afternoon was guarded, the mood was not happy, and I was not sitting in Room 227 at East High School finishing up my normal teaching day.

I found my mind racing in every direction possible. I thought of fond memories from over the years and what I thought would be happening the following week. I thought about loved ones who had passed in my lifetime and began to seriously consider the fact that I was perhaps on the cusp of joining them in the hereafter. I thought about fellow church members who had passed and their loved ones. The more I stressed over the idea of going to bed later, the deeper I sank into gloom. I remember clearly wondering to myself if before they passed they felt the same painful feelings and perhaps heard the same ominous conversations. My state of mind really sucked. I could not talk, or for that matter move freely, and all I could contemplate was that perhaps things were heading in the wrong direction.

If there were a few things I would suggest in this situation to help the patient, it would be to again plan on being there for the patient holding their hands when they fell asleep and staying with the patient all night until they woke up. This awakening could happen in the middle of the night or in the early morning. The closer loved ones can be to the patient to make them feel that they are not alone the better.

On Monday I had not become aware with clarity that I had already died six times that day. All I realized was that every time I woke up, I felt worse. Worst of all, I was agonizing over closing my eyes for the last time. Life that late afternoon was way below my feelings when the Chicago Cubs walked off the field in their final game in 1969.

I was completely aware that my wife, daughter, parents, siblings, and in-laws were all attempting to say the right thing and boost my spirits higher, but within seconds of supportive thoughts I would look at where I was and what I was hooked up to and I would immediately lose the warm fuzzy feelings.

The last agonizing memories I have of that first day were the moments leading up to my falling asleep. Even today, with a little emotional feeling, I remember how I felt that night. I remember thinking about my kids and wife and praying to myself that I would awake again tomorrow and see them all. I remember fighting every urge to sleep. I fought with all I could not to close my eyes.

I wanted Stephanie, Brandon, and Jennifer all to be in the bed with me watching TV together and relaxing like we had so many times before. I hated the fact that I still could not speak and could not convey my wishes. The last thing I remember doing that night before going to sleep was shedding just one more tear. My world went painfully dark at that point.

Flashbacks are something the heart attack victim might very well have to experience. As I sit in Room 227 writing this book during my lunch hour, I find myself very emotional right now. For the first time since my heart attack the flashback memory of waking up early that morning just came back into my thoughts. I feel like it just happened—not a good feeling. I have not told my wife about this to date because it has been too difficult for me to relive the moment. I am not sure what time it was in the early morning, but I did wake up just once. I was alone and painfully without any of my loved ones there to hold my hand in reassurance. The room was dark and cold. I thought I was dead. I closed my eyes and cried. Wow. That was extremely difficult to write.

For loved ones of heart attack victims, please insist on spending the first two nights with your loved ones who are scared and worried about what they are going through. Hospital administrators reading this book, please encourage at least one loved one to be there all night for easy hand access. Please.

"You were way dead."

Chapter 8

As the next morning arrived, I remember opening my eyes and getting very excited about everything around me. It was a huge relief that I did indeed wake up. Until I started to feel my sore chest, the catheter taking care of my bodily functions, the tube down my throat, and finally a tube up my nose, I actually felt pretty fantastic. Very quickly Tuesday morning everything the doctors had attached to me that I found myself so hating was removed. I can remember like it happened just an hour ago the relief I felt hearing the statement that it was time to remove all of these not-so-pleasant objects.

If I could wish for something different on that Tuesday, it would have been to wake up with at least one loved one nearby. The memory of waking up early in the morning thinking that I had died and was alone remains even today very fresh in my mind.

At the growing realization that I had "made it," my disposition improved very quickly. Pretty quickly after nurses removed the medical attachments to my body I started to talk to everyone whom I could. If there were some changes I would make for that day there would be a few. The first would be to limit visitors to only family members and loved ones. No more. The mental fatigue from reliving the event and the numerous times telling the story is just too difficult and unnecessary. While I did not want to say, "No, you can't come into my room," for those there to wish me well … I should have. I very much appreciated the teachers, administrators, and students who showed up, but by the end I found myself emotionally exhausted.

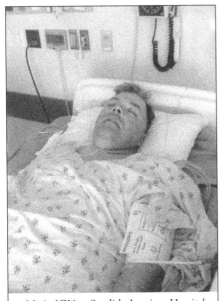

Me in ICU at Swedish American Hospital

Tuesday I will remember as the day when I inserted my foot into my mouth several times and to this day regret what I said. It was Tuesday when I made some of meanest and ill-advised statements I could possibly have said. To this day I am not quite sure what made me blurt out some of the feelings I conveyed, but I wish that I had held back. I can only blame the fact that for the previous thirty-six hours I had almost continuously asked myself, "Why me?" and, "What did I do to deserve this?" When I saw loved ones with what I thought were controllable issues that could bring on a heart attack, I became scared to death for them and their children. I just wanted to say to them, "Please, for your children, please make better choices. I don't want to lose you as a sibling, and I know your kids don't want to lose you either." Within seconds of expressing my feelings I felt like a real jerk.

One thing that I have learned during the last nearly twelve months since the heart attack is that blunt communication inhibitions are sometimes limited when speaking. Since that really bad day in March, I have found myself being much more blunt or frank about my opinions. I have found myself being a great deal more frank with people, in my opinion. There have been times when frankness is welcome and others when it could be a real problem.

I have been trying to curb the reflexive responses with greater restraint and fewer rude results, but since the heart attack it has been much more difficult. The problem with holding back reflexive responses to questions or observations is that the conversations become fewer and less spontaneous. The additional problem that I have found is a tendency to avoid people altogether as I have found myself doing on Sundays, not wanting to be blunt or hurt feelings. As a result of avoiding conversations or limiting my opinion in existing conversations, loved ones start to worry about state of mind and/or depression. To say it best, the feeling of being between a rock and a hard place is a very, very real feeling.

Although I was really enjoying finally having the ability to speak and listen to loved ones, I found myself internally wondering how quickly my doctors could visit and tell me what the heck was going on. In between the numerous visitors, my wife and I started to reflect on the previous day's events. I could not help but feel that she was not telling me everything about the status of my diagnosis. As much as I thought I wanted information about the entire situation, I realized after getting some of the information that I was starting to be bothered by the information and the seriousness of the situation at hand. Perhaps it was a prime example of getting too much information too quickly, as I started to feel a little emotional depression.

During short conversations with my wife, daughter, and son on Tuesday, I reluctantly gathered superfluous information without specifics related to my health. My memory of the moment was that we were all waiting for the cardiologist who took care of me to visit my room. I have no doubt in my mind that my wife was telling me more about my health status than I remember, or perhaps my mind just refused to absorb the rather serious problems I was about to start dealing with on a day-to-day basis.

The importance of writing down any questions related to the situation at hand is critical. Doctors are busy people, especially cardiologists. Every question, big or small, should be written down to discuss. Do not assume that the doctor perhaps will be back later for more question and answers. Presume that they will not. Ask all the questions that you have, even the smallest. Don't hold back any questions for later, because you may not get that chance.

All loved ones and family members should be part of the generation of the questions. If possible have loved ones and family present when the cardiologist visits. Accomplishing this loved one and family list of questions will go a long way in eliminating stress for everyone, including the patient. One designated questioner to ask all questions versus rapid fire from all directions can help eliminate the stress of the moment.

It was not until my cardiologist finally visited my room for the first time, on Tuesday, that I was able to learn firsthand just how bad things were and what I had been through in the previous thirty-six hours. After he checked my vitals, I could no longer put off asking the questions that I needed to know the answers in order to understand the "How bad is it?" question. At the time I found myself guessing my state of health. I honestly felt that my situation was on a scale of one to ten about a six. I had emotionally prepared myself for a confirmation of my thoughts related to the scope of the situation.

Reflecting back, I pretty much counted my eggs before they were hatched emotionally. I was big-time wrong. I went into the conversation thinking that what I had was a minor heart attack with the side-effects and ramifications disappearing perhaps by next week so I could go back to my normal way of life. After all, there have been numerous articles that I have read about catching the heart attack early and avoiding the "big one." Prior to my conversation with the cardiologist, I was actually mentally preparing lesson plans for the following week, trying to figure out how to catch students up with a lost week of school while I quickly recovered from a slight heart scare.

I approached the conversation with the cardiologist with the bravado of a bull in a china shop. First of all, let me say that my cardiologist answered my questions in the manner that I honestly wanted him to convey. There has been a great deal said about the bedside manner displayed by many in the medical field and how it could generally be much better. In this instance I disagree; the bedside manner shown by my physician was just what I would have hoped to experience (if I had to be a patient).

The news was not good. He provided me with all of the background information related to heart attacks that I asked him for, and for that I was very appreciative of his forthrightness. After all the background questions related to heart attacks were answered, the inevitable questions related to the seriousness of the heart attack I suffered were all that were left for me to ask. Parts of me dreaded the questions; other parts kept on saying get 'er done … and how bad could it be? In the end I just had to ask. The answer was something that will be forever burned in my memory. Given the chance for a do-over I would have liked to be holding my wife's hand and surrounded by family.

As the cardiologist began to speak about the seriousness of my heart attack it seemed like his conversation started to really slow down. He became very deliberate in what he was conveying regarding my questions. The more deliberate he became, the more nervous I felt. Finally, with no more background information available, he professionally conveyed just how serious or close I came to not celebrating another birthday. "You were not just a little dead ... you were way dead."

Words cannot begin to describe the total and complete loss of words I experienced at the time. I was stunned. I tried not to let on that I was stunned, but I was. He then went on to discuss what he had to do to save my life. He spoke of the six times that my heart had to be shocked. He spoke of how much of a miracle it was for me to live through a 100 percent blockage of the left anterior descending artery and that survival of that extent of blockage was rather infrequent. He spoke about the fact that while I was feeling pretty unlucky for having the heart attack in the first place, I should really be thankful for just how lucky I was to still to be alive.

It was then that the cardiologist conveyed the alias name given to my type of heart attack. It seemed like slow motion the way he said it; but only because it will be burned in my mind forever. "You had the type of heart attack that people refer to as the *widow maker.*" That statement hit me like two tons of bricks. WOW!

The cardiologist went on to talk about my ejection fraction (EF) percentage, which was 35 percent. He went on to explain that ejection fraction is the fraction of blood pumped out of a ventricle with each heartbeat. Sensing my concern, he went on to convey that the average adult male has an EF of 50–65 percent. While I felt horrible thirty seconds earlier, I felt better with more understanding of the situation.

The challenge I learned regarding the EF was to strengthen my heart to a point where my EF might someday again be 50–65 percent.

The doctor went on to explain more about why my percentage was indeed low. The more I learned, the more I realized just how much work I had in front of me to accomplish. To be honest, however, I had my doubts that anything ever happened and that this was all just a horrible nightmare. I have always been able to struggle through adversity in my life. I kept on telling myself repeatedly that next week that I would return to class first thing Monday morning.

Something I did not take into consideration regarding my approach to the doctor telling me my medical condition for the last thirty-six hours was the feelings of my wife, daughter, and son. Perhaps they knew better than I did and realized just how bad things were just thirty-six hours prior. While I appreciated the doctor's forthrightness, my family did not feel the same way about the manner the doctor chose to convey my situation. While I was lying there in stunned silence trying to think of something funny or sarcastic to say given the situation, my family stood close to me, upset, based on what I saw in their eyes.

Bedside manner on the part of the doctor is very important to the patient and loved ones there to help. Doctors are brilliant people, but they should never for one second treat the patient or loved ones with any less respect than what they would expect or want if the roles were reversed. This "flip-flop" rule should be enforced by the loved ones in a diplomatic but firm manner. Take the time to walk the doctor out of the room away from the patient first. At this point the last thing a patient needs is unnecessary avoidable stress. With diplomacy, propose to the doctor the "flip-flop" idea and have the doctor convey information without belittling family members or loved ones for their medical questions.

Expect the doctor to answer all the questions necessary and hopefully written down. If the doctor seems to be in too much of a hurry to leave without the questions being answered, get between him and the door and provide him with an obstacle to exit or contact a nurse to slow down the doctor's quick exit. You are paying big money for his time. Make him earn it. You should not feel as though it is okay for him to hurry out and see another patient. His one job and only job at that moment in time is the patient he is with.

Ongoing discomfort

It was day three in the hospital when more chest discomfort started to settle in. The discomfort I am speaking of was not the excruciating pain like I felt just three days earlier but rather soreness and yet another small nagging problem. It was day three when my family, doctors, and nurses started to notice my extreme coughing. It was not the cough that hurt but the soreness in my chest from being shocked six times, and perhaps the intense chest compressions. The coughs came from out of nowhere. They just happened. They did not originate in the throat like most coughs but somewhere quite different.

It was not my mission to be a bad patient. With every cough my chest felt uncomfortable, with pain. With the pain came a shortness of patience about the situation, and oftentimes that frustration transferred via curt statements to family. The more I coughed, the more it hurt. I found myself holding my chest tightly with each cough, trying to reduce the percussion effect of coughing to my chest. Soon the doctors agreed that I was probably the proud owner of pneumonia, which was caused by aspirations shortly after I woke up on Monday as a result of the trauma to my system. While I was already taking a bevy of medicine, the pneumonia added a couple more to that list. While the doctors would like to have seen me go home on Wednesday, I remained in the hospital until Friday because of the pneumonia and risk of further complications.

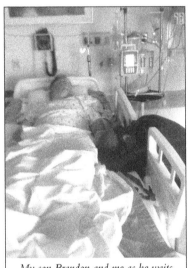

My son Brandon and me as he waits for me to wake up

Here is where I find that my conscience must admit to my failing in the hospital. Shortly after I was diagnosed with pneumonia I was given a deep breath funnel that helps mitigate the complications from pneumonia. It was a purely stubborn decision on my part. My chest hurt with every cough. The last thing I thought that I would like to do would be to take large deep breaths and then blow hard. It's not like I avoided it completely, but let's just say I would have given myself a C for a grade at best. The stubbornness associated with the breathing pump was much like my stubbornness toward accepting the fact that I was not going to be in the classroom like normal the following Monday. I'll be there and I won't get pneumonia. It is just a small cough. FYI: this approach is very much a bad approach to take the first week after the heart attack.

Pneumonia, I learned later, is pretty common to heart attack sufferers depending on the health and age of the patient. Don't for one second assume that the normal run-of-the-mill case of pneumonia is normal when it is combined with first suffering from a heart attack. Since my heart attack I have been astounded with the number of articles that I have read about heart attack sufferers surviving the heart attack but then dying from the complications of pneumonia. Don't underestimate the possible ramifications of pneumonia. Blow on that breathing tube with great conviction and an almost religious persistence. That approach will pay huge dividends. Okay, my conscious is now clear. Do as I say and not as I do.

Shortly after the doctors made their visit to my room the arrival of the specialist responsible for the first stage of rehab shocked my world. I had been told the day prior that the specialist responsible for the first rehab stage would visit on Thursday. I kept on thinking that I was that tough guy who was dealt this really bad deck of cards. With extra effort it would go away as fast as it arrived.

The rehab nurse first outlined what I would be asked to perform the first day. As she told me the plan I thought to myself that it would be a piece of cake. Let's get real—that is something that I could normally do: walk down the hall and perhaps up a flight of stair with no effort whatsoever. I walked with the rehab nurse down the hall.

When she challenged me to go down the other hallway and up the stairs and then back down the stairs and then ultimately return to my room, I did it like Sir Edmund Hillary (the first person to scale Mt. Everest) had scaled Mt. Everest. I badly wanted life to return to normal as quickly as was possible. I felt like Sir Edmund himself during the walk and stairs, but afterwards I felt like I was a marathon runner just finishing twenty-six miles. I was completely exhausted as I returned to the room, and I remember the depressing feeling once I realized that my physical reality had definitely changed.

I wanted to prove to my daughter, son, and wife that I was the big strong father and husband they had known just a few days prior. I did not feel like some healthy forty-eight-year-old man but instead a husband and father who could be considered in fact a complete mess. I was weak and tired like a man thirty years older than I actually was. The more I found myself attempting to be Sir Edmund, the more I realized just what I could not do. I failed to realize at the time that success or failure at stage one of cardio rehab was not based on climbing Mt. Everest but rather the fact that I was merely alive to look at Mt. Everest and attempt the first few steps.

I had admittedly been a very lucky person through this entire nightmare. On Thursday afternoon, after completing day one of phase one, the rehab marathon, I was sitting down resting when I quite unexpectedly and shockingly started to have some very intense shooting chest pains. At first they were an annoyance and could be ignored, and then after a few pains I started to get a little worried. That worry was also showing on the faces of both my wife and my daughter. While they tried not to show the worry I could see right through their "don't worry, Pat, it will only make it worse" look. It was then that the nurse told me to take a nitroglycerine pill. Earlier in the day we discussed how the nitro pill worked to open every blood vessel and artery, when they should be used, and finally why they should be carried at all times for the rest of my long life.

I have seen movies where the heroes take the nitro pills and do not miss a step. This seemed like a Hollywood fantasy that was not to be replicated in my room on that day. Let me tell all of you reading this book not to minimize the physical effect of taking the nitro pill the first time. If you ever want to replicate the effects of taking that first nitro pill without actually taking the pill, have someone take a big thirty-four-ounce baseball bat and have them hit you upside the head with it. Enough said. I have learned since that day that the physical effects of taking a nitro pill are not as profound after the cardio rehab regime is established. Fitness does amazing things to the body.

God willing I would never have to take the nitro pill ever again (regretfully that has not been the case). The heart pain went away, but everything from the neck up hurt. It was something that I will never forget.

The next couple of days were relatively uneventful compared to the taking of the nitro pill. I continued to cough more and continued to have great discomfort in my chest with each and every cough. Medically, I started to get more and more frustrated as during the last few days in the hospital I started to realize that my once-fit body was not bouncing back the way I had anticipated just a few days prior.

The more I considered the slow progress, the more agitated I became to my family. I realize now that I was completely in a state of denial. I would pose the question for doctors and professionals that perhaps the last day in the hospital should include a visit from a heart attack psychologist in order to help minimize or perhaps alleviate patient and family anxieties post–heart attack.

IT'S TIME TO GO HOME

CHAPTER 10

As Friday arrived, after being there for four days, I, like most patients, got to the point where frustration set in. I was tired of the room, the food, and the smell. Worst by far was the inconvenience that they did not have satellite service and could not get the Chicago Cubs games. The hospital was great, the doctors and nurses were fantastic, and I will forever owe Swedish American Hospital more than just statements of appreciation as I know they saved my life, but that did not change the fact that I was ready to return to my normal life.

My lifelong dream home.

As much as I was very excited to leave the confines of my medically safe hospital room, my mind started to think about the "what-if" scenarios of doom and gloom that related to where I live and its distance from the hospital. I love where we found our dream log house in Rock City, Illinois. We have been able to send both of our children to one of the best schools in Illinois as far as I am concerned. My wife found her dream position as a teacher at Dakota High School in the theater and music department. We have been able to own seven beautiful horses on five gorgeous acres of land.

Most of all I have cherished the downtime of the commute between home and work, which is about thirty-five minutes. As I said earlier, I was living the perfect life. Unfortunately, dreams sometimes contain complications. The complication in this situation is that if I were to have another medical emergency, the rural location where we live would likely not afford me the same positive outcome due to the close proximity and luck I had a few days earlier.

What I considered a "normal life" all changed at 8:45 AM on March 31, 2008. I realized as I was getting prepared to leave the hospital that although I was excited to go, I did not want to be even five yards from the hospital, let alone thirty-five minutes. As my wife pulled the car up to the front door I felt my emotions beginning to change. It was then that I started to get very nervous and very paranoid about leaving the safety of the hospital. I found myself mentally checking all my body's feelings, checking and double checking if I felt any chest pain or perhaps another heart attack. I knew at the time that it was silly, but nonetheless I was very nervous about pulling out of the hospital driveway. I found that with every mile that separated me from the hospital I became more and more nervous. I remember distinctly thinking that I was acting like a little a child without his security blanket. The hospital had become my security blanket.

As we left the city limits of Rockford, I found myself looking at my watch and watching the second hand move as time now seemed to last forever as my wife drove me home from the hospital. I could not believe how long it took us to get home that first time. I found myself searching out all the for-sale signs listed on homes as we drove what seemed to be a two-hour trip home.

In actuality, the trip was no greater in length than the hundreds of times I traveled it each and every day to work. On this trip, however, I felt my chest becoming tight and my breathing a little more difficult from time to time from the sheer anxiety of leaving the hospital. Emotionally, the heart attack patient is very complicated, to say the least. All thoughts seem to be happening fast forward as life seems to be changing more quickly than ever before. Silly and stupid thoughts often find their way into their heads, and a random laugh or smile may surface as the patient is internally trying to create upbeat and goofy thoughts to create an upbeat or positive disposition. For me the last thing I wanted to do was accept the depressing thoughts and not try to find something to be happy or to laugh about.

Horses of tranquility

Chapter 11

As we drove down our driveway with the tree-covered canopy, I was both scared and thankful in the same breath. Most people own cabins in northern Minnesota or Wisconsin to escape from the hectic day-to-day challenges that affect daily living. I, on the other hand, was fortunate enough to find what I best knew as a Lincoln Log home throughout childhood that happened to be situated in northern Illinois. As we drove down the driveway I realized just how lucky I was to live in this secluded rustic Daniel Boone–Davy Crocket type log home. I found myself laughing inside about my paranoid feelings during the trip and just how laughable my thoughts were.

Bailey, Mocha, and Sydney

I started to realize that where we lived was the very best place I could live. Like a cabin in Minnesota or Wisconsin, our place would be a great place to begin mental and physical recuperation. As I entered the house I thought to myself how close I came to never returning. I know thoughts of leaving loved ones were thoughts that should have been considered, but at the time I could not help but appreciate the home we considered our dream house. As I walked through the house I looked around the kitchen and living room with greater appreciation than I had less than a week earlier.

I walked to the rear sliding doors to our deck and found myself hoping and praying that I would see at least one of our horses. Due to the fact that I was not sure if the horses had gotten the "coming-home script" that I had written in my mind, I was prepared for the fact that they may be exactly where I did not want them to be on my arrival home from the hospital.

I would suggest very strongly that every heart attack victim find something in their life that provides for a degree of tranquility or perhaps simplicity. In my instance, that tranquility takes the form of my horses. They are gentle giants. They are huge but as gentle as a mouse. They are smart but only communicate via movement. I find myself totally at ease and calm when I ride my horses. I find it intriguing that horses generally do not judge and love unconditionally.

Some horses can have issues, but generally they are a result of human beings screwing up and doing something they should not do to a horse. I have been fortunate to have incredible horses. I am able to daydream and solve all the problems that exist while sitting on the back of a horse and riding.

On this day, my first day back, my horses were once again brilliant in how they rehearsed this self-written script that I had coincidently written also. They were not quite lined up looking out over the wooden fencing, but they were at least there all lined up to take turns drinking at the water trough. I watched them for a few seconds, and for those few seconds I felt great.

As I walked away from the horses that day I remembered one of the promises that I had made myself as I lay in the cath lab knowing that I had put my wife in the terrible position of owning too many horses. The moment after I felt great comfort at seeing all my horses I realized that I would have to make some very difficult decisions as quickly as I could in order to satisfy my personal promise to my wife. The comforting feeling of seeing my horses had quickly changed to a level of sadness.

While we had initially purchased two of the horses for our children, for whatever reason my great kids never really caught the same excitement I had in owning horses. While they very much enjoyed owning the horses, they more or less enjoyed brushing them or feeding them carrots from time to time rather than riding. Over the next seven years the Fox horse herd had ballooned to seven horses. At the time of my heart attack we had six.

Brandon and Stephanie feeding the horses

I remember being very proud of both kids during my first several weeks after getting home. I was so very relieved when I realized how fantastically they had taken on the unfamiliar responsibility of horses during the first days and weeks of my home recovery. While half kidding they did communicate to me that it was not something that would last forever. My kids taking care of the horses took a great deal of pressure off of me.

During my week in the hospital I constantly found myself worried about my horses. Taking care of the horses for the last ten years had become a daily routine. While my children loved to feed the horses treats and to brush them they really had not taken the next step in taking care of the horses daily.

I had all the confidence in the world that my children would step up, yet there still remained a level of apprehension. Without asking, both of them stepped up and took care of every horse's need. While they did not tell me they had fun, I am quite sure they enjoyed it as much as I had for ten years.

My first days home ...

Chapter 12

It's strange how children react to an emergency. As I lay down on my bed in the loft of the house I wondered just how the rehabilitating program was going to progress. At this point my wife Jennifer was doing the best acting job I could expect her to perform. If awards were possible she would have received an Academy Award. My wife did everything she could to not appear overly stressed out or worried, much like she had in the hospital. I could see a huge level of worry in her eyes. I could see that she was emotionally exhausted. I badly wanted her to relax and stop worrying, but I realized that, given my current health status, that wish was unobtainable.

The discomfort that I was feeling as I lay in bed was worrisome at best. The chest tightness and soreness had dissipated slightly while I was at the hospital, but only slightly. The pain level with each and every breath was still in the area of about a five. Each breath I took was something I could not describe as routine or without discomfort.

While the lingering effects of pneumonia made breathing difficult and seemed to get worse at home, I am sure it was a reaction to being thirty-five minutes away from the hospital and trained professionals. With every cough my chest felt tight and very uncomfortable, much like it did at the hospital. In the hospital I had prayed that at least some of the pain associated with my hospital visit would stay in the hospital versus following me home.

As much as I love my family, I was very worried that something would happen to me physically such that they could not provide adequate emergency help. I was petrified as to how much pressure I thought the family was under, given my situation and the miles away from the hospital and medical assistance.

Given what had happened on Monday with little warning I became rather worried about the time between our home and hospital. In our town we are blessed with an outstanding volunteer ambulance company that is both quick and professional. The problem is that they could never respond quickly enough to save my life if I had the same massive heart attack and only had five minutes to reach the hospital. I failed to rationalize everything that the cardiologist had done to my heart with the angioplasty and heart stent. I know this worry had nothing to do with my family, but nonetheless they were the ones who would have to deal with the situation if it arose.

I am not sure if my wife, daughter, and son got together and talked about who would babysit Dad and when, but quickly their roles started to exhibit themselves. My wife took on the role of the general or lead shadow who would direct everyone but also make sure everyone was accomplishing everything in order to keep me from any worry of any type.

Stephanie took on the role of immediate shadow. She took care of my every need almost before I asked. The importance of having someone who can oversee the consumption of medications is critical when the patient arrives home. While I really tried to focus on the medications, my mind was not as sharp as I would have liked. Having someone to act as medicine caretaker is critical and very important the first few days home from the hospital. The aches, pains, and general body discomfort very much require a primary shadow or helper to assist the recovering heart attack patient.

Brandon, my son, took the "waiting in the wings" role. While he conveyed his willingness to help frequently, he focused on taking care of the horses with his sister and being tough. As she had done so often for many years, my daughter lay next to me talking and bonding. In this instance I realized very quickly that this was not a conventional bonding between father and daughter. It seemed with every breath (and I don't think I am exaggerating) she asked me if everything was okay and if there was anything she could do for me. With every painful cough I could see her feeling my discomfort. I badly wanted to hide the fact that her dad was not the strong dad that I had been less than a week earlier. I felt very vulnerable and helpless, and I did not like that feeling in any way.

Throughout that first day at home I coughed and coughed as a result of the pneumonia, and my family seemed to feel the pain with every disconcerting cough. It was that first night when I started to feel shooting chest pains. The best way I can describe the feeling is that it felt much like someone pushing a small but very sharp pin into the heart area of the chest. Simultaneously, with the sharp pain I felt an uncontrollable snapping contraction of my bent arm into the chest and the snap of lowering my head to my chest accentuated with a quick gasp. The pain lasted only milliseconds and was gone almost before it arrived. Nonetheless, it was painful and very worrisome. As much as I wanted to take some pill that would make these pains subside—I realized that the nitro pill would alleviate the pain—stubbornly, I did not want to take the nitro pill for a second time.

I realized during a later visit to Northwestern University that indeed I was overly stubborn that first night at home and should have taken the nitroglycerin pill to alleviate the shooting pain I felt that night. My advice regarding the nitro pill would be to take it when you feel an elevated and lasting chest discomfort.

I did everything I could to hide these shooting pains from my already very worried daughter who was lying only inches from me, but quickly I realized that I could not. These pains seemed to accelerate in their frequency and then without warning cease for a half hour at a time. I rationalized that they were not continuous in nature so I did not have to worry about them too much.

I tried to refrain from telling my daughter, but no matter how much I tried to hide them she realized that they were happening. Again, I felt helpless and weak in the eyes of my daughter. I did not like this feeling, and I became very frustrated with the situation.

As I lay in the bed, I felt the ever-more-frequent feeling of frustration. I did everything I could to focus on the good things in life and how lucky I was to still be around for my family, how much I loved owning a log home, and finally my other lifelong dream of owning horses.

I wanted to give my daughter a kiss on the cheek and say thank you and carry on with life as if nothing had ever happened. The more I thought about the fact that it wasn't that easy, the more frustrated I realized I was getting. I tried to watch TV with my daughter and struggled through my frustrations, but the fairly frequent shooting pains of a needle into my heart brought me back to the present.

As I lay with my daughter making small talk I consciously started to think about the idea of going to sleep. The more I considered sleeping, the more I started to come emotionally unglued. It took all my emotional strength to avoid inadvertently communicating to my daughter that I was worried about not waking up the next day and how upset that thought was making me feel. The more I felt the shooting pains, the more I worried about being at home alone in just a couple of short days. I knew at the time that these feelings were invalid and probably really stupid, but nonetheless they continued to creep into my very emotional thoughts. I made up a lame reason at the time, but I asked that Jennifer and Brandon join us for a few moments.

All of them, including my daughter, spoke when they came upstairs, but to be honest I don't think I heard a word they were saying. While I did respond, my mind was flashing back to when they were much younger and my wife and I were new parents and how special that time was. I almost lost it completely when I thought about the question of not waking up the next morning. While I once again acknowledged to myself that the thoughts were silly, they vividly existed.

One thing that my daughter did that I would suggest very strongly is that she created a pill chart for taking my prescription medicine. When I first came home from the hospital I was on at least ten different medicines, and they can be confusing unless organized.

Hospitals or a family member should create an Excel spreadsheet that clearly provides for a detailed routine for taking the prescribed medicine.

It was very difficult for my wife to leave the house both Friday night and Saturday for the school musical she was directing at her school. During my hospital stay my wife and made the decision that she would not direct the school musical for both nights. As much as I really did not want her to leave the house either night, for selfish paranoid reasons of insecurity, I convinced her otherwise.

My daughter would be placed in a very bad position of being

alone with her dad and being responsible for my health in a manner that she had never faced before. I remember how nervous she was when my wife prepared to leave for the performances. My daughter did everything she could do to mask her nervousness, but I could see that she was about half as nervous as I was, given the situation.

I am not to this day sure if the phone calls by friends and other ones who knew my wife's obligations provided my daughter with any sense of comfort, but she made it through like I knew she would. It was that night, more than any other night in the last several years, that reminded me just how lucky I am to have the daughter I have. I was very proud of her; she had grown up to be a pretty incredible young women who when put into a difficult situation could rise to the occasion.

In fact my daughter did a fantastic job of taking care of my every need. I would suggest that no one person be put in the position of sole responsibility for the first few nights. The assistance of at least one other person or perhaps a support team would have been helpful, if not only mentally for the heart attack victim, but physically if in fact an emergency had arisen.

At the time I felt like a real maladjusted heart attack patient, but every time she had to go downstairs to get food or drink I actually got worried that something would happen while she was gone. Stupid, I know, but at really emotionally difficult times, strange things run through the mind.

It was on Tuesday when my son, Brandon, took over my primary care during the day while my wife, Jennifer, went back to work. I could tell how nervous he was the first week, but just like I expected of him, he did an incredible job stepping in and taking care of his dad.

Bedtime nightmares

Thoughts of going to bed for the first several nights at home were not what I would call "*Mr. Rogers' Neighborhood*" pleasant moments. (I know that invoking *Mr. Rogers' Neighborhood* is a little corny, but in this instance it is appropriate once again.) If I were a betting person, I would have bet good money that my blood pressure and anxiety went up with every second the clock ticked closer to bedtime.

The first couple of nights at home I agonized over the idea of going to sleep and woke frequently during the night. I am not exactly sure what prompted the flashbacks that started the third or fourth day at home, but each night, memories related to that horrible heart attack seemed to slip back into my consciousness.

I found myself suddenly remembering the sights, feelings, and emotions I had experienced. Some of these thoughts would surface prior to sleeping, and others caused me to awake with a startle. My wife was the best at handling these flashbacks. I would convey fragments of memories, and she would do her level best to fill in the sometimes very fuzzy memories.

We discussed the phone call she received from the ambulance and how she felt about my bad back. My heart broke when she told me how difficult it was to be told that it was not my back but rather a heart attack. The more she told me about that moment, the lower my heart sank. I found myself actually superimposing myself into the situation as an invisible bystander as she spoke on the phone to the paramedics. Later after she fell asleep that night I cried. The scenario of her taking the phone call and how she handled the long car drive played through my mind in a continuous loop manner.

She told of the eighty-miles-per-hour drive from Rock City to Rockford and Swedish American Hospital that her best friend Annette navigated and her highly emotional feelings in transit. She discussed and I listened to her narrative of how she communicated the bad news of my heart attack to my daughter, son, and parents.

We discussed the timeline of doctor and nurse conversations I had the first two days. I realized that nearly everything I had thought to be reality actually happened, but in a much different script sequence. We talked about the very painful NG tube inserted in my nose and why it was necessary. We spoke about the very real feelings of suffocating as a result of aspiration. I told her for the first time of my emotions when I woke up in the ICU as I thought I was a vegetable and was paralyzed completely. She told me about who visited the hospital and when. She communicated her conversations with doctors and nurses and how close she was to losing me.

The first week the flashbacks and conversations took place at all times of the night after what was normally bedtime until the wee hours of the morning. My wife was very understanding and loving the entire time. The more we spoke, the more I felt enlightened about the entire event. There were times during our conversations when my heart broke, as I learned about the conversations my wife had with my parents as she broke to them the news of my heart attack. About other conversations, I felt a sense of relief for knowing what really happened that day versus what I realized now was my somewhat fragmented recollections. In some respects it was a good feeling to know what happened for everyone on that day. I realized during these conversations just how much family tends to pull together during difficult times. I started to again appreciate the closeness of the family I grew up with but also the family that I have now. I thought about just how lucky my family was to have pretty much avoided many experiences like the one I was experiencing. I fell asleep thinking about my brothers, sisters, and parents and hoping that none of them would ever have to experience what I had a week prior. I told myself that I would do whatever I could do to convince all of them to get checked for heart disease as now there was a family history.

Flashbacks are something that I understand now are very normal for heart attack patients as they have been through a traumatic experience. The manner in which my wife answered the questions was brilliant. She gently answered all the questions that I asked of her. I think it was brilliant that she did not provide any information that I did not first question. I honestly believe that she understood the need to not rush memories back into my mind. She was right. Almost one year later some of the more disturbing memories are only now being remembered.

First weeks and months home

Chapter 14

If there were upsides to the entire event, one of them was the time I was able to spend with my son. While we have always been a close loving family, it was incredibly therapeutic to have my son there to hug and speak to during that first week home. Thinking back, I realize that God provided me with an opportunity in that if this was going to happen at least it happened during the very short window when both my daughter and son were able to be there for me. Reflecting on the moment, it would have been much more difficult if both of my children could not have been there for me to hug on demand.

In my situation, where all my family was able to be home for me, there was no need for an alternative method. For those families who don't have the convenience of being there for the heart attack patient there needs to be an alternative. In today's world where technology has provided for skyping (video teleconferencing) on laptop computers, other technologies should be considered to facilitate family connections.

The shortness of breath and a chest that was continuously

uncomfortable the entire first week out of the hospital was not something I ever want to repeat. My chest hurt from the six defibrillator shocks and the compressions that I received. The coughing and shortness of breath originated from my unfortunate aspiration in the ICU. More than anything else that entire week I struggled with the idea of staying awake. I found it difficult to accept the idea that something so physically traumatic caused me to feel uncontrollably fatigued more than I had ever experienced before.

I sometimes don't realize that perhaps my family makeup is slightly different if not radically different from many families. Our willingness to provide a big hug or a kiss on the forehead is something that we do not give a second thought to. The ability to say that we love each other has always been something we don't hesitate to convey. I would suggest that the ability to provide a hug and provide the random "Love ya" is something that every heart attack patient needs during the difficult days of recovery.

While my daughter, Stephanie, reluctantly went back to her life in Chicago, my son, Brandon, accepted the primary support role during the day. While my son may not have been an enthusiastic caretaker of the family horses, he was nonetheless a great standin.

While my son took care of my every need during the day, he took a secondary role to my wife in the evening. The backup support is something that I think every primary care family should have at their request. No one person should feel all the pressure or responsibility if at all possible.

In his backup role the first week after the heart attack, Brandon found it a priority to set up a new cell phone I had received the week before. I realized later that he was working on a special project that this book started out with, by writing a letter to Disney regarding a favorite new shirt I was wearing the day of my heart attack.

The importance of family for a person who has been affected by the heart attack should not be minimized. My wife, daughter, and son were incredible in their support during those first few weeks at home. With the exception of those first two days when my daughter thought I should return to the hospital when I would double over with the shooting pains, they were incredible. Their ability to support, nurture, and randomly provide the necessary hugs was a big reason for my successful rebound from that really bad morning of March 31.

Reflecting back on the situation where I felt needle-like pins being pushed into my chest, I think hospitals should provide a hospital staff member to spend time with family members to discuss the possible physical and emotional needs of the patient when everyone returns home.

The assumption that just because the patient has left, bad things could not happen could be a fatal assumption, and family members should be provided with possible scenarios with preferred actions to take. If the hospital does not provide for this education it is up to family members to probe for "what-if" scenarios prior to hospital departure.

As several weeks passed, my physical limitations seemed to improve slowly and rather methodically. The importance of having a loved one near the patient for as many days after getting home as possible is very important. The emotional support I felt having my son there just to talk with from time to time was priceless.

There were days when I felt great and nearly ready to get on with life and yet other days when I found that I could hardly get out of bed physically. The fatigue factor is something that should not be underestimated. While it can be said that no two heart attacks are the same and no two recoveries are the same and the need for the support from loved ones in my opinion are critical for successful long-term recovery. On those days when I would unexpectedly feel completely worn out from pushing it the day before by walking around the house or spending time with the horses, it was incredibly comforting to know that I had someone there to help.

The time Brandon spent with me before he was to return to Disney in Florida was priceless. The emotional support he provided in the early weeks of being home was incredibly helpful as often I had no idea when I would be exhausted from over-activity.

It was not until shortly before Brandon was scheduled to return to Orlando to continue his dream of a career with Disney Company that he and I had a disagreement about something that I can only describe as "insignificant." While I may have some weak moments along the way, it was not until Brandon and I had the small disagreement that I finally had what I would describe as my total emotional venting and breakthrough of unspent emotions related to what we had just been through.

As a result of our disagreement during the day, I completely lost all composure and humility and emotionally collapsed. I had never done that in front of my wife, daughter, or son for that matter. I found myself very embarrassed by showing my son that I was weak. One moment I found myself very embarrassed to show my son the weakness I had just showed him; the next moment I felt a sense of positive emotional release. Until that moment when I emotionally finally lowered my "tough guy" facade that I had built since the day my life changed, I really did not feel a release of pent-up negative emotion.

The day following my "meltdown," Brandon indeed felt bad about the disagreement we had, and I truly hope that he understood that the emotional meltdown or collapse had little if anything to do with the disagreement. I cried loudly and uncontrollably and at great length. I don't think I had ever collapsed like I did that night. To this day, Brandon and I have never spoken of that night again. Jennifer and Stephanie were never told about that night; perhaps it was just something Brandon and I considered "a man moment."

In the days that followed that emotional night I came to realize that Brandon indeed had yet another purpose after my heart attack. In addition to being my son who took care of my new cell phone the week of my heart attack and being there to provide support for the last several weeks I realized he had done so much more. That night I realized just how close a family we were and that indeed Jennifer and I had been successful in raising our children to be caring and willing to help regardless of the situation.

The night I emotionally vented about my anxiety and displeasure with the heart attack Brandon lay next to me and I cried like a baby as if he were the dad and I were the child. He held me tight, much like I had done so many nights over the previous eighteen years as he grew into the special young man he is today.

TELEVISION SHOWS BECOME DIFFICULT

The televisions shows *E.R.* and *Grey's Anatomy*, long Thursday night staples of entertainment for the family, became difficult at best to watch as they were often intertwined with heart attack commercials. I found that commercials for Plavix and Lipitor, which often played during those two shows, really bothered me, and I often had to leave the room. I felt my heart become heavy when I watched as the hospital gurney in the Plavix commercial following the heart attack victim everywhere he traveled throughout the city.

It seemed like every episode in *E.R.* and *Grey's Anatomy* included at least one heart attack and two chest-cracking scenes. Perhaps that is an exaggeration, but nonetheless I found myself emotionally able to watch fewer and fewer episodes of either TV show.

One of the more heart-wrenching dilemmas about suffering a heart attack for me was the reflection of friends or loved ones who died from similar causes. I thought about friends or acquaintances who had suddenly died, whom I now presumed to be victims of the widow maker. The more television I watched, the more I remembered an old friend whom I had learned a great deal from: Jon Lundin. Jon was a local man to Rockford, Illinois, who worked as president of the local Goodwill Industries for years.

He was incredibly active in and around Rockford attempting to not only improve the images of Rockford but also to improve the lives of those less-fortunate families or individuals who had run upon bad economic times. Jon's other passion was working to improve opportunities for special needs citizens living in the area. Jon was truly someone who changed many lives in many ways. Jon had become one of the mainstays of Rockford and its proud history. I am not sure why the thoughts of his sudden death busied my mind, but perhaps his sudden death mirrored so much of what I myself had experienced.

I found myself seeking everything I could read or hear about his death. I found myself listening intently any time there was a TV or radio story related to heart attacks. Any time there was a story about heart attacks, heart disease, or strokes I found myself completely consumed, anticipating the airing of the stories. I realized at the time that I had become a compulsive TV watcher for stories related to these topics, but I could not stop learning from the experiences other people were having. It is surprising all the satellite channels that air news stories about those topics. Some of the stories had happy upbeat endings; others the opposite.

When the sudden death of Tim Russert was announced as I was watching the nightly news, my world was completely rocked. I vividly remember that I was lying in bed when I heard of his untimely death. I was devastated by his very sudden and dramatic death. If anyone had attempted to talk to me when the announcement of his death hit the TV, I would not have heard a word of the conversation until the news story had ended. I so wanted to hear that he died for some other reason than the widow maker, even though the circumstances of his death were so similar to what I had experienced.

I am not sure why I wished to hear the cause of his death; I guess because I so badly wanted to hear someone else surviving a similar heart attack like the one I had suffered. I surfed every news channel that night to find out specifics of his death. Every channel, every news person, spoke of just how special Tim Russert was and how he had lived his life. It became even more personal when the newscasters spoke of his relationship with his family members. It was then that I felt a very close connection, as I felt a kinship of sorts about my family and how close we were to each other and obviously how close the Russert family appeared to be according to the news stories.

It was *The Larry King Show*, which featured Tim Russert's cardiologist and Tim Russert's son, that brought time to a stop for me. I know it is perhaps a little shallow, but I could not take my attention from the television. If I had checked myself for breathing during the news stories I don't think I was. I was that anxious and nervous to hear from a medical professional just what caused Russert's premature death.

As news anchors spoke about the minute-by-minute story of the moments leading up to Tim Russert's cardiac arrest, I found myself getting more and more anxious with every second. The more they spoke, the more I sensed they were dancing around the details. Then, with one word, I realized that Tim Russert had suffered the same type of heart attack I had, with the alias of "the widow maker." As soon as I heard those words, my heart dropped and I emotionally felt depressed and overly emotional once again. I cried as the lights went out as I went to bed the night they disclosed Russert's cause of death.

The more I watched TV, the more I found myself noticing

commercials or news stories associated with the quality of life or psychological difficulties of depression. Some of the commercials talked about the post-partum blues and how depression can be a significant problem. Ironically, the number of e-mails I received in my school e-mail account regarding mental health and the winter blues seemed for once to be apropos in my life.

Although these monthly health e-mails from the district went out to all teachers, I got to the point where I thought they were targeted toward me specifically. I honestly arrived at the point where I almost expected to see e-mails about depression or mental health. The more ads and commercials I saw and listened to, the more I started to wonder if that it could happen to me.

Emotionally Difficult

The subject of this chapter is by far the most difficult to write regarding the first year of my recovery. I have always considered my mental disposition to be strong and capable of adjusting to all circumstances thrown my way.

I never contemplated several things ever happening to me. The first would be a heart attack, and the second would be fighting depression. My entire life I had never spent more than a moment or two reading newspaper stories or watching stories on TV related to the farfetched idea of depression. Even after suffering the heart attack and hearing many medical professionals speak to me about the possibility of suffering from depression, I internally laughed and said thank you, but it could not happen to me.

The incomprehensible consideration of ever dealing with depression only crossed my mind in October when it seemed that the Loveable Losers (aka the Chicago Cubs) would blow the post-season once again. As I worked through the difficult rehab program and my forever-changed life, I began to realize just how much my life had changed.

The friendships that I had established for the previous forty-seven years were found to be very important in this new personal chapter. The occasional phone call or text message from Tim, our pastor, or Elizabeth, an associate in ministry, or Craig, one of our church musicians at Christ Lutheran Church where my wife also works and we are members, conveying their support were often perfectly timed to when my spiritual and emotional feelings had dropped.

The ability of my parents and in-laws to phone me at just the right time was eerily timed perfectly, as if they were sitting next to me and knew when I needed an emotional boost. The occasional e-mails from my sisters, Susan and Kathy, conveying their hopes and prayers were indeed needed from time to time. I am not sure just how my brothers, John and Jimmy, had a clue when I needed my big or little brother, but somehow they both knew just what to say and when to call or stop over to provide needed support. Everyone's genuine concern for my life and health was sincere, to say the least. Although I did not want anything to change for me post–heart attack, I started to realize that wishing for no change was just not good enough.

Of great importance was my overwhelming desire for everything to be the same when it came to my immediate family and loved ones. I would literally stay awake at night trying to talk myself into being that "endlessly happy go lucky (EHGL)" dad or friend that most everyone used as a description for my day-to-day disposition prior to my heart attack. As time wore on, I reached the point where I would consciously realize that I no longer had that EHGL disposition.

There were times during the average day when I would realize that my frame of mind really sucked. I consciously realized that my mind was in its own little world and that sometimes things going on around me seemed to be disconnected from my existence. There were times when those feelings really scared me into thinking of myself as a "space head"; something that I never thought I could or ever would use to describe myself.

In reflecting back to practically any post–March 31 day I realize now that I had been missing a great deal mentally. My friends and loved ones had been great in so many ways, but almost every person asked either me or my wife, "What is wrong with Patrick?" At first when I would hear that question first- or secondhand, I would say simply "nothing" or something like "nothing; I feel great." As time passed, that question was posed more and more often.

On nearly a daily basis my daughter and I would speak to each other on the cell phone, and I got to the point where I could expect the follow-up text. "Dad, are you okay?" I love my daughter very much, but I got to the point where I acted out an upbeat disposition during our daily calls. I just did not want to defend my disposition after the conversation.

In time, my feelings became more and more sensitive to the same question being asked on what seemed to be a more frequent basis. I began to realize that I was snapping back at the person asking the question; often at people who really cared about me. The more frequent the question, the more often I found myself avoiding the question by withdrawing more. This only exasperated the situation of people thinking something was wrong with me. The frustration of not feeling "on my game" combined with the fatigue I felt defending my psychological status to everyone close to me finally wore me down until I started to accept the simple facts.

I had read over the years heart-wrenching stories about people on depression medicine doing bad things and the side-effects some people have when on depression medications. When I mentally added those stories to the medications that I was already taking for my heart attack, I became very concerned about medical addictions and side-effects. I found myself doing research on the Internet in private, attempting to find out the correlation between heart attacks and depression. I badly wanted to be the exception to the correlation and not one of the statistics.

I was able to fight the symptoms, or so I thought, until school started in the fall of 2009. It was then that I realized that I was in fact trying to fight or get over symptoms that were beyond my control. I finally came to the realization that my loved ones were not fabricating their concerns for my mental state of mind. They were only concerned about my mental health, and I finally started to accept the fact that I was in fact fighting the D word: depression.

The emotional toll that can be brought on by negative feelings or frustrations can be significant. There were times and days when I would leave school emotionally exhausted and spent. The more frequently I felt those negative feelings, the further I found myself sinking emotionally and physiologically.

In the end I started to listen to family members and loved ones when they spoke about my poor disposition. After a great deal of prayer, I decided to see a doctor and face the fact that depression had taken my best mental fix and beaten me.

With the help of Cymbalta, a depression-fighting medication, my life has become brighter yet again. Now that I have successfully arrived at my one-year anniversary since the day of my heart attack, I have found myself more invigorated in my day-to-day life thanks to a more solid frame of mind and physical workout routine.

It is important to understand that anti-depression drugs are not the total answer to fighting the side-effects of depression. Anti-depression drugs should be considered as supporting staff in fighting depression. Another supporting staff player should be a good non-invasive heart attack psychologist.

No less a critical component of a successful heart attack recovery is a workout routine that is followed religiously. Many heart attack patients never make to their second heart attack anniversary because they fail to maintain the workout schedule.

I have learned over the last twelve months that heart attacks can be considered on many different levels of seriousness. Some victims actually fail to realize that they even had a heart attack. In my case, the dying six times is considered to be very traumatic. I have also learned over the last twelve months that there are many levels of depression. I have learned that heart attacks like mine can actually carry with them Post-Traumatic Stress Disorder.

Suffering a heart attack is something that I never thought would happen to me. Suffering depression after suffering a heart attack is just that much more incomprehensible. The contemplation that I could ever suffer from Post-Traumatic Stress Disorder as a result of a traumatic heart attack is completely crazy. The reality, as it is today, is that all the previous improbable or seemingly impossible scenarios or thoughts are in fact reality.

I have found that understanding the fact that these problems are possible is half the complication of recovery from a heart attack. I would suggest that Internet research into all the possible problems associated with having a heart attack is critical. The more you know about what is possible, the faster you can mentally rebound.

CARDIO REHAB

For much of my life I have always thought of myself as a pretty physically fit person. The concept or thought that I would be or could be a candidate for a really major heart attack was something that never crossed my mind. During those days leading up to the cardiac rehabilitation (cardio rehab) program, I still mentally maintained a certain amount of bravado or perhaps stubbornness.

I maintained a positive mental mindset that I still had the ability to perform a simple workout as a forty-eight-year-old. While I did feel a little tired while resting at home after the "event," I still psychologically maintained that it was just a small bump in the road. Ultimately when I called upon my body to start physically working hard, it would athletically answer my call and respond as mentally requested.

As I prepared for cardio rehab I found myself doing mental weightlifting. I just kept on thinking to myself how bad can it be? While I realize that friends are perhaps not the most medically in the loop, I spoke with many who tried to downplay or I guess minimize the effects of my heart attack by saying, "If it was really that bad they would have cracked you open." While they were well intended in communicating their opinions, I probably could have received better advice from a fortune cookie.

Brandon and the Chipmunks during a happy visit to Disney World

As I performed the mental calisthenics preparing for the cardio rehab I did the best I could with my positive mental attitude. Like my son conveyed in the opening letter to Disney, I found myself listening to the SpectroMagic CD. The CD had been purchased during our last Disney World visit, and the music reminded me of visiting my son at Disney World and all the fond memories.

The SpectroMagic music is special to me for several reasons. The only place anyone can hear the SpectroMagic music is at a Disney theme park during the spectacular and amazing SpectroMagic parade. While I listen to the CD I am able to transport myself to the main street of Disney World. Disney World to me represents the best warm fuzzy place on the earth.

Walt Disney in his creativity was able to transform what many of us believe to be common day-to-day surroundings into a utopia on earth where no bad exists and no sadness exists (unless the little one in the stroller is really tired) and more importantly is a place where people

Stephanie, Minnie, and Jennifer at Disney World during a happier family time

are able to forget life problems and, at least for as long as the visit, live without negative thoughts.

In addition to the Disney CD, I found myself trying to take the frame of mind from people I admired for their tough-guy persona, whether real or perceived. I found myself daydreaming and thinking about tough guys like Walt Disney, John Wayne, and Clint Eastwood. I found myself trying to listen to music that would get me over the "event" mentally ASAP. I was convinced prior to rehab that I could get better just by "bucking up" mentally. I discovered that the song "Live Like You Are Dying" from Tim McGraw really hit home and made me feel mentally stronger.

Looking back at the attempt to "buck up" and in hopes that it would miraculously enable me to get better, I realize now that I was crazy and naïve at the time. While I did physically feel tired from time to time leading up the cardio rehab, I thought at the time that to a certain extent it would be a piece of cake. For the baby boomers reading this book, I found out during and after the first day of rehab that Evel Knievel jumping the Snake River Canyon was simple compared to the reality of that day.

During the first session of cardio rehab I was told that many heart attack victims cut short or in many instances decide to eliminate the idea of cardio rehab from the recovery because "things will get better on their own." When I was told that information, I thought to myself, well, if that is the case then I am sure I might be able to do the same thing. Let's just participate in a few of the rehab sessions and then I can prove to my wife and kids that I could just skip the remaining sessions and let things get better on their own.

Getting ready for the session and hooking myself up to the electrodes to read my heart functions I began to understand just how serious and important these sessions were for those who really needed them to recover. In my delusional mind I used the word "those" to describe the weaker and in-poor-shape heart attack victims who would need cardio rehab. In no way would I have ever placed myself in the same category. Two words sufficiently describe the "those" characterization I used: foolish and naïve.

It was less than forty-five minutes later when my entire life changed for the worse yet again. With each station in the rehab program I became more frustrated, exasperated emotionally, and physically exhausted. After the completion of the final station on that first day I sat on the stationary bike attempting to catch my breath and clear my mind to avoid falling off. I just laughed at all the really stupid thoughts I had just forty-five minutes previously. I actually looked back at the desk where I had checked in for the session and remembered every thought that went through my mind at the time related to "someone else" or "those people" who actually needed cardio rehab.

I am sure that Maggie (my coach) and the other ladies, Tracy and Kathy, realized how over-confident I was when I entered the facility that day and how really crappy I felt as I staggered to leave. They were true professionals and avoided making any humorous statements or even a small laugh, but if they had I would have deserved it that day. I realized as I sat preparing to leave that I had seriously underestimated my physical health status.

Never in my entire life had I been so mentally and physically more completely humbled and exhausted than in that first thirty-minute cardio rehab session. I am so very thankful that my wife refused to let me drive myself to the first session. I nearly argued with her so much that first day about taking me to rehab that I almost won. The need for my wife to drive fell once again under the category of stubborn pride. The emotional needs on my part to feel I could "handle" things like I did prior to the heart attack were very real and strong emotions.

Historically, two or three hours of intense training had only begun to create the level of exhaustion I felt that day. My wife Jennifer took me home that day from cardio rehab, and I felt like a total wimp. My mental frame of mind dropped like a rock as I began to realize just how much damage the heart attack had caused. On returning home that day I think I slept twelve hours straight as I felt completely mentally and physically exhausted.

The professional women rehab specialists that I worked with and others were incredibly helpful but demanding in the cardio rehab program at Swedish American Hospital. If every heart attack patient could have the opportunity to work with the professionals at the Swedish American cardio rehab, I am convinced that every heart attack victim entering rehab would be as successful as I was.

There are many incredible hospitals around the world, and I am sure that most, if not all, either have a cardio rehabilitation facility attached or perhaps a contract with a local facility that staffs cardio rehab professionals. The importance of utilizing the facilities should not be underestimated.

The life and recovery of the heart attack victim hinges on the dedicated usage of the facility by the heart attack victim. The percentages of those who suffer a major heart attack and die within one year are substantial for those who ignore rehab opportunities and just "buck up."

For those who choose to utilize the rehab opportunities, the chance of a long life is greatly enhanced. For victims and loved ones … please take the time to rehab the heart.

In the weeks following that first session of rehab I found myself attacking the rehab sessions like I attacked coaching. Each and every day I convinced myself that I had a defined purpose to attend and finish each session better than I had the previous session.

There were a few setbacks during the sessions when I pushed the envelope just a tad bit too far. Thank you Tracy and Kathy for not giving me too much grief for pushing the arm exercise during one session until I foolishly found that I needed to gracefully lie on the floor and momentarily pass out from over-exertion. It was embarrassing that I could not finish with class that day, but I did realize just one more thing about rehab and how physical limits can quickly arrive.

As the number of sessions passed I found myself feeling stronger and stronger. The cheerleading group of Maggie, Tracy, and Kathy was relentless in their support of my efforts. For at least the sixty minutes I spent working out I mentally felt very strong and fully on my way to recovery.

With every session that I left feeling great I left with the opinion that I could soon start riding my horses. My wife would still see a little fatigue resulting from every session, and she felt that any horseback riding was a bad idea and should wait just a little bit longer.

Until I was able to actually go back to school and teach she felt it was a bad idea to get on any horse and regret the decision. The rehab sessions were providing me with physical strength and also a mental strength that I thought would be ready for the last ten days of school. As the day approached I was both nervous and excited to return.

Driving by the school during the running of some errands I found myself starting to get rather upset. The memories of the heart attack just kept flashing back into my thoughts.

Much like my feelings on the first day at cardio rehab I thought the first day back at school would be simple. Once again, I was completely naïve and the day went horribly. I completely underestimated the emotional side of returning. With the emotional mistake of teaching that day came a physically exhausting feeling like that I felt after my first cardio rehab session.

It was truly special to see all the staff, fellow teachers, and the students whom I badly missed, but as I got up into my truck in the teachers' parking lot that day at the end of school, I realized that I would be unable to return for a visit the next day as I was completely exhausted. For the next ten days I worked only half days and finally the last two full days of the school year. The fatigue of teaching those last ten days, even half days, became very frustrating.

I badly wanted to feel like I had prior to my heart attack. The substitute teacher the school found to fill in for me was outstanding. I unfortunately felt as though I had abandoned the kids, and it was a frustrating feeling.

When I was able to complete several more rehab sessions I was finally able to convince my wife that riding a horse might be good therapy.

FIRST HORSEBACK RIDE

CHAPTER 18

Jennifer riding Bailey

My entire life I have loved horses. It took me until I was forty to finally purchase my first two horses. I paid a small fortune to become a John and Josh Lyons certified trainer in 2004 to better understand the physiological needs and emotions of a horse. John and Josh Lyons are in my opinion the two most "tuned-in" professional horse trainers on the earth today. As a result of better understanding horses, I have discovered that I am often more relaxed when riding.

Combining this history with the fact that I was unable to get on a horse during most of the spring due to doctors telling my wife that riding a horse would be a bad idea (too bad they did not just tell me) and I found myself on a daily basis watching my horses outside, spending extra time feeding them, and enjoying the occasional brush. As time passed it almost became painful that I could not ride. I don't think I could have handled getting one more *Trail Ride Magazine* in the mail without snapping.

Finally, after my wife relented and permitted me to ride in our round pen for a few minutes, I felt like a million bucks. The downside of the round pen ride was that both my wife and I both realized the physical toll it took on me. I was tired. Okay ... I was exhausted.

It was not until several weeks had passed of cardio rehab at Swedish American Hospital that I finally was able to convince the boss (my wife) that I could ride Sydney, one of my horses. This time I was able to convince the boss that I could ride outside of the round pen. We decided to load the horses and trailer them to Lockwood Park; a Rockford Park District park located on the far west side of Rockford, Illinois, just twenty-five miles away from the "Fox Ranch." Both Sydney and Bailey, the horse my wife was going to ride, jumped in the trailer with the enthusiasm of the official first real ride of 2008.

The trail ride that day was truly fun and beautiful. The ride, however short, was uneventful and indeed a wonderful feeling. We finished riding about 10:00 AM as we thought it would be a good idea to ride early in the day and relax and enjoy the rest of the day. Both horses rode exceptionally well for the first ride of the year.

I finished loading the tack (horse equipment) and went to load the horses. Bailey, like before, nearly jumped into the trailer. Sydney walked to the rear of the trailer and suddenly acted like the world's meanest shadow had invaded the trailer. Thirty minutes later, after attempting to bribe, beg, and ask politely Sydney to enter the trailer peacefully, the decision was made to try plan B ... at least that is what I told my wife. The problem was that I had absolutely no idea what plan B entailed.

Due to the fact that I had spent a great deal of money on learning about horses and their psychological makeup, my wife looked to me for a brilliant solution to Sydney deciding to draw her line in the sand and not go into the trailer. It took about fifteen minutes sitting on a nearby picnic table and looking at my watch to concoct a plan B.

With a voice that sounded confident, my plan B was conveyed. Within seconds my wife thought I was having another "mental event" and conveyed her opinion that I was in fact crazy. Plan B was to saddle Sydney and ride home. I conveyed my plan as I looked away from her as I knew I would laugh as I conveyed the plan. I think for my entire life I will remember what I was thinking the entire time I tacked up Sydney. I just kept asking myself, am I totally insane?

As I mounted Sydney for the long ride home, I pretty much decided to look at the ride as perhaps an emotional sign that having a heart attack could not define me as a person. Until that day I had failed to find something that would convince me that I was the same strong person that I always had been.

The first six hours of riding northwest to the Fox Ranch made me wish that we had not moved quite as far from Rockford as we did and seemed to last for days. It was during the last four hours that I began to think of the ride as a journey.

My mind started to go to strange places, thinking about western cowboys like how John Wayne would handle an entire day's ride. I felt for sure that John Wayne would have laughed at the challenge and embraced the long ride as just another day in the saddle.

To finish off an already memorably uncomfortable day, Sydney provided me with just one more twist. Roughly three miles from the Fox Ranch, she conveyed that I needed to walk her the final miles of the "journey."

As the clock struck 10:00 PM as I walked her up our driveway and then into the barn to remove her bridle, saddle, and blanket from her, I realized that I was totally physically and emotionally exhausted.

For the next two days I was nearly bedridden from total mental and physical fatigue. On the second day after my life-changing ride I was scheduled for rehab at Swedish American Hospital cardio. While every effort on my part was put forth the following day at cardio rehab, I found that I could not even get through the first rehab phase that day. I felt like I had taken a large step back physically and emotionally. I felt humbled and whipped at totaling failing to "man up" from horseback riding as I returned home feeling exhausted and needing a very long nap.

After my long nap I had to face the music and talk to my wife about the cardio rehab like I had every other day. After first saying that I had in fact finished the entire session, I later reluctantly came clean and admitted I failed to finish. The look I received from my wife that day was rather painful but worth it when I considered why I had failed to finish the session. To be honest, it was worth the feeling of fatigue and exhaustion, as I had no regrets for following through with plan B. Accomplishing the "journey" was a huge mental accomplishment.

On the third day after completing the journey, I walked out to the pasture and put a halter on Sydney to begin working on re-educating her once again on how to enter the trailer. As I walked her to the trailer for the first review lesson on trailer loading I walked with a distinct level of soreness from riding the "journey."

As I walked Sydney to the trailer, I mentally prepared for what could be a lengthy trailer-loading lesson. With great confidence, I decided to just walk with Sydney directly without hesitation into the trailer, much like I attempted just three days earlier. With only a heartbeat of hesitation as she lifted her first leg, she stepped into the trailer as she followed me straight in without any resistance. I repeated this exercise several times with no hesitation whatsoever.

John Wayne may have been able to ride his horse for long days, perhaps twenty-five miles alone. In this instance my wife indeed did not desert me and tell me, "See you at home." She followed with the trailer every inch of the way, not letting me get out of her ever-vigilant sight. She followed me or drove ahead of me in my big truck, pulling my big trailer a few hundred yards at a time. She did this every inch of the way along the twenty-five-mile, ten-hour journey. While I did feel a sense of accomplishment, I very much appreciated my wife being with me during the journey. While the journey was something I felt I had to accomplish, I also found myself very nervous along the way when I would think about recovering from a heart attack.

One thing that I learned from my horse-training education is that in fact horses are very intelligent, almost clairvoyant animals. On the day of the "journey" I came to believe that in fact my horse, which had historically literally jumped into the trailer during the loading process, had decided that that day would be my day to learn from her. She was correct. It was.

As a direct result, that significant event and the emotions involved provided an important aspect of my healing. The journey provided me with the emotional confidence that I was capable enough to accomplish something and the ability to prove that I could; all a critical part of recovery.

DECEMBER BOWLING BALL

One byproduct of having a near-death experience times six is that one tends to read up on as much information as might be available on the Internet or on medical TV. I read about the symptoms for recurring problems associated with heart attacks. I became pretty knowledgeable on symptoms that might represent the onset of another heart attack.

While I found myself more educated as to the symptoms, I found myself mentally asking myself how I could possibly differentiate between similar symptoms. Like anything else in life it is difficult to differentiate pain from discomfort or chest discomfort from common everyday random chest feelings.

As I discovered in October, not all shooting pains and numbness of the arm are heart attack related. To describe the feeling of heart pain and numbness as frightening is an understatement at the very least. The mind can do funny and maddening things sometimes. Jennifer was equally concerned the more I felt the heart pain and numbness. If the pain and numbness had subsided within a few moments I would not have mentioned the moment at all.

Unfortunately, the scare started with the heart pain and the shortness of breath, following by the numbness in my left arm. The total elapsed time from the beginning to the end was over two hours. The drive to the Swedish American Hospital became a needed trip once again.

The staff at the emergency room was as incredible on this October day as they were in March. They were professional, polite, and motivated in terms of speed. The more tests they did as they evaluated my condition, the more I started to realize that they were finding nothing to be concerned with regarding heart problems. Mentally, I felt a great deal of frustration as I most definitely felt the symptoms, but medically there was no confirmation of them, and it really bothered my inner confidence.

Everyone from the cardiologist to the nurses spoke firmly that I should not ignore this set of symptoms. Given my rather serious heart history, symptoms like what I came into the hospital with should never be ignored, especially since the symptoms that presented themselves during my heart attack were not conventional or typical symptoms.

I spent the night at Hotel Swedish American, and the medical professionals did everything they could to determine the cause of my scary feelings. As diligently as the medical staff tried to find something wrong, there was nothing to find and no explanation to offer for my symptoms.

One of the frustrations associated with recovering from a heart attack is that sometimes recovery momentum can be interrupted psychologically if not physically. While the physicians were unable to find any problems with my ticker in October, the question of understanding the "true symptoms" of a heart attack continued in my mind.

While the inner anxiety continued from October, I physically felt better and better. I religiously power-walk with one of my daughter's dogs, named Morgan, which she had loaned to me during my rehabilitation. We both religiously power-walk three or four times each week for forty minutes each time around a roughly one-mile oval, within the village of Rock City, Illinois.

The need to steadily increase cardiovascular strength by increasing the heart rate for an extended period of time is critical to rehabilitation. Ultimately, with the increase of cardiovascular strength the ejection fraction rate of heart function will also increase.

In power-walking around Rock City with Morgan, I found myself pushing myself more and more with every mile lap. In order to really get the most out of the art of power-walking it is important to perform some serious stretching of legs, arms, and the upper body. While some workout routines are artful and pleasantly appealing to watch, the cardiovascular power-walk would not be extended the same description.

The cardiovascular power-walk is odd and goofy looking, kids laugh and mimic, and ultimately it is very tiring when done correctly. The best cardiovascular power-walk requires long steps, arms flailing front to back, and most definitely a nice pair of power-walking shoes.

Life and power-walking around Rock City continued almost religiously, requiring the home treadmill during bad weather, into December with little or no concern about heart attack déjà vu as I felt I was doing everything I needed to do.

In early December came the day of the bowling ball moment. I know that physicians often attempt to convey clinical descriptions of symptoms, but for me utilizing the image of a small women's bowling ball sitting on the center of my chest was at the time the best description.

It started while I was teaching eighth-hour class. With no relief of pressure on the center of my chest through the entire ninth hour, I started to get very concerned about the real possibility of another heart attack as the conventional symptoms of sweating and light-headed feelings presented themselves occasionally.

I did everything I could not to show the students that I was concerned in any way for my health. I attempted to joke with my students during both classes. The longer the bowling ball stayed on the center of my chest, the more I lost focus on what I was saying in class. I have no idea why I did not take a nitroglycerin pill during this episode; perhaps it was how much I did not like the last time I took a nitro pill.

The more the bowling ball stayed on the center of my chest, the more nervous I became. On reflection, I was nuts for not getting in contact with the school office staff to initiate an emergency medical situation to get me to the hospital quickly; in hindsight, I was pretty stupid.

Emotions play a large role in recovering from a heart attack and understanding when discomfort is real or just a passing bother. While the hospital professionals did their best to convey that I should be concerned about discomfort, the desire on my part to not be considered a "the sky is falling" type of heart patient was foolishly very important to me. As I stubbornly walked around the classroom that day in December, I just kept on repeating to myself, "This is not happening, and it will go away quickly."

I did everything I could to joke with the students during the class but also with students in the hallways leading to the office. As much as I tried to joke, the bowling ball would not go away. By the time I arrived in the main office I had reached a level of concern that I had not felt since March.

As soon as I mentioned to the office staff that I was looking for the school nurse, the 911 speed dial went into action. The more I felt the bowling ball that day in December, the more I became scared that it was reminiscent of my heart attack the previous spring. In March, I failed to feel the conventional heart attack as I felt only shooting pain in both of my shoulder blades. This December day I felt what I believed were the conventional heart attack symptoms. The longer the bowling ball lasted, the more my anxiety escalated. The bowling ball never started at the center of my chest but to the right of my heart and never moved to my lower abdomen or up to the larynx area. It just stayed in the middle of the chest.

I attempted to minimize the bowling ball feeling by trying not to contemplate the eminent health threat by joking with students or other teachers around me, not telling them what was going on physically with me. As much as I attempted to make small talk and jokes with students and administrators around me, the feelings of a potential heart attack arriving soon would not dissipate.

In addition to the bowling ball symptom I began to break into a sustained cold sweat, dizziness, and the feeling of physical weakness. For the first time, my symptoms very much mirrored what are believed to be conventional symptoms of a heart attack. Suffice it to say that Hotel Swedish American Hospital became my home for yet another night. Once again the entire staff was professional and proficient in every test they performed.

While I was incredibly relieved that I had not suffered another heart attack, I realized that I became more introverted and reserved on a day-to-day basis. Loved ones and friends became more and more concerned with the passing of each day nearer to the Christmas holiday.

While a concerted effort was made to mentally turn my psychological disposition around, I found it more and more difficult to accomplish. A great deal of effort was made to put a positive thought process on the Christmas holiday, but regretfully the outcome was not as successful as I wished.

With February came hopefully the final symptoms I would feel related to what I would think was another heart attack. The symptoms were not identical to December but were similar. Once again, in February I faced yet another exercise in understanding the difference between chest twinges and valid heart attack symptoms.

While there was no bowling ball this time, the shortness of breath, sweats, and light-headed feeling arose one more time. The complication this time was that during these moments I was also experiencing trouble in the classroom with students who had decided that failure was acceptable. This added stress of students accepting failure only added unwanted pressure in my day-to-day life.

Prescription Drugs

Chapter 20

Never in my wildest nightmares did I ever think that my prescription medications would be one of the biggest challenges associated with recovering from a heart attack. Not only do prescription drugs have a primary target effect, but many have a secondary and sometimes a third effect, what may be a physical and emotional effect that may not seem to have anything to do with the heart. My wife, Jennifer, did everything she could to oversee my prescription intake, but without a degree as a doctor or a pharmacist that challenge was complicated.

Following a doctor's orders regarding the taking of prescriptions is very critical. Paying attention to your own body is at some point more critical. I have learned that doctors prescribe drugs based on their best understanding of drug effects based on medical history. It would be simple if all bodies had similar makeups and responded to prescription drugs the same, but that is not the case. The need for loved ones to pay attention for signs of drug conflict is critical. Flushing, rashes, increased unexplained fatigue, and excessive aches and pains of joints can be signs of negative drug interactions. These symptoms, I learned, are real and should not be ignored regardless of where I might have been when I felt them. For me some of these symptoms happened before bedtime and during school, which only complicated the entire situation.

There were times when my wife would make a phone call to her sister Martha, who is a pharmacist in Kansas, to decipher the complicated medicine interactions. When I was asked what prescription drugs I was taking for the heart attack I would often respond, "One from each letter in the alphabet." After spending time looking up the prescriptions on the Internet for information on them and learning from the doctors and pharmacists we became very knowledgeable on the drugs.

Between March 31, 2008, and the one-year anniversary, I experienced both the great healing powers of prescription and the frustrations of negative drug interactions. I personally think drug companies should provide frequent flyer or perhaps frequent buyer incentives for the people who purchase their products. If the prescription drug makers of Zocor, Protonix, Plavix, Ecotrin, Altace, Toprol, and Cymbalta are by chance reading this book, please sign me up as a frequent buyer points participant.

If Plavix needs yet another spokesman to be a star in a commercial that touts the shock of having a heart attack at a young age I am here for that also. Perhaps I could be found by the movie makers to costar in the next big-screen cowboy movie. *Okay. That was an example of what went through my mind when I experienced a negative drug interaction.*

The unwanted experience of having a heart attack and fighting through it to a full recovery often takes many twists and turns. Dr. Saberhwaul and his team at Swedish American Hospital were given the knowledge and gift of saving my life on the fateful day March 31, 2008. I have a million reasons to appreciate their skills as doctors and cardiologists.

The convenience of having my cardiologist on staff for all my visits to Swedish American Hospital was comforting indeed. They were professional and thorough in all they did to provide me with adequate information.

Sometimes help in recovering from a heart attack can arrive in unforeseen moments. For me it was at my thirtieth high school reunion. One of the things that weighed heavily on my mind the week I suffered the heart attack was the organizational meetings for my thirtieth high school reunion. I questioned if I was going to be able to organize the reunion and ultimately if I was going to be up to attending the event.

As I have said several times, there are sometimes unexplainable moments when strange things become emotional motivations for living and being there for friends and loved ones. For me I found myself driven to work hard in rehab to be in the best physical shape for the reunion.

It was during that reunion when I reconnected with many friends from the class of 1978 at Rockford East High School. I discovered that one of my classmates, Anne, happened to be a doctor at Northwestern University Hospital in Chicago. After the reunion I learned from Anne that there are significant differences between invasive cardiologists and non-invasive cardiologists in methods of treating the heart attack patient.

I discovered how important it was to understand the virtues of each specialist and what each brings to the table for specific states of recovery. My high school classmate's referral to a brilliant cardiologist at Northwestern University Hospital dramatically changed my physical and emotional progression in a huge way.

Sometimes recurring symptoms combined with mental frustrations spawn the need for more information or a second opinion. With the move to Northwestern University Hospital in Chicago and a better understanding of the strengths associated with a non-invasive cardiologist I became enlightened to the direct relationship between having a heart attack and the reality of fighting psychological depression. While I found myself fighting the incomprehensible thought that depression could ever happen to me, I realized along the way that indeed the idea of depression should be considered reality and nothing to be ashamed of emotionally.

I met with Dr. Rigolin at Northwestern University Hospital regarding my recurring symptoms, and she enlightened me as to just how related depression and heart attacks and disease really were. In a way, that close correlation was comforting to me. With all the psychological fighting that I had done since my heart attack, I felt a huge rush of acknowledgement for my emotional feelings. I guess for the first time since my heart attack the idea or realization that I was for the first time not feeling guilty or ashamed about suffering from depression finally provided comfort.

Northwestern believes that there is a strong correlation between suffering a heart attack and symptoms related to depression. This commitment to the correlation is exemplified by having on staff a psychologist who specializes in that relationship. It was some time after my first meeting at Northwestern University Hospital in February when I started to again feeling chest pressure and discomfort in my heart that I started to get very nervous about my health yet again.

It was then that Dr. Rigolin called me late on Friday night and told me to check into Northwestern Hospital the following day. Given my recurring symptoms she felt it was time to find out why symptoms kept presenting themselves. In addition, EKG results from my October visit to Swedish American Hospital and one taken at Northwestern in February provided concerning comparative results.

The medical professionals who staff the emergency room at Northwestern should be given a world award much like those at Swedish American Hospital deserve. I have never visited a hospital that was more professional in attire and communication than Northwestern University Hospital. I found the idea of being a patient at a teaching hospital to be an incredible experience. As a teacher professional, I very much admired the doctors as they communicated to their students specifics about the procedures they performed on me.

While a visitor at Swedish American Hospital I received nuclear stress tests and EKGs on each of my visits in October and December, and I was to receive an EKG and an angiogram at Northwestern University Hospital.

I would encourage any person reading this book not to just accept with blind faith the opinion of just one person regarding your health. Take the time necessary to seek out a second opinion on your medicine or physical well-being. If you are having symptoms that are continuing without explanation, I would say to find that explanation with another cardiac professional. No hard feelings.

The results from my angiogram from Northwestern combined with the communication from my new cardiologist and her staff at Northwestern University Hospital changed my life completely. Since March 31, 2008, I have not felt as excited about my physical health as I did when I walked out of Northwestern on February 10, 2009, after spending three days at Hotel Northwestern University Hospital.

The insight that I have gained from the cardiologist at Northwest University Hospital regarding the correlation between heart attacks and depression and physical feelings and real heart attack symptoms has completely changed my outlook and understanding of the science of experiencing a heart attack and the difficulties of living through it. Because she practices at a teaching hospital, she and her professional staff have the God-given ability of communication. What I discovered also about a teaching hospital is that they have the innate ability to be better listeners.

As a teacher I have always had the opinion that if a teacher or professional is unable to communicate the specifics of a project or a specific job then they really do not have a clear idea what is involved. The team at Northwestern was exceptional in their knowledge and communication as they had an over-the-top ability to dissect each part of the procedure into small parts and communicate it in medical terms to the interns and in plain English to me and my family.

Going forward I have all the confidence in the world that the Northwestern University Hospital team will provide me (us) with all the healthcare needed given their approach to cardiology research and care. The importance of finding a doctor whom you feel comfortable with is a huge factor in recovery.

It is critical to find a doctor who is willing to answer your medical questions without clock-watching or holding the door open, waiting to leave. Make sure the family and the patient are comfortable with the doctor, as a common positive feeling is tantamount to whole-body recovery.

While my visit to Northwestern did not enlighten me entirely as to why I was still having an occasional symptom, I did come to a couple of important conclusions as a result of the Northwestern visit. The first would be to realize that in fact my symptoms are real and should not be minimized. The second is that every person at the age of forty-eight is probably feeling the same occasional symptoms. The difference is that a person who has suffered a heart attack is much more in tune with their bodily feelings. That is not a bad thing.

The benefit of getting an objective second opinion provided me with a much-needed addition to my daily prescription regiment that has greatly reduced any concerning symptoms.

High School Teacher

One objective that remains a continual struggle is the minimizing of really big ups and really big downs emotionally. As a teacher I have found that goal to be difficult if not impossible to accomplish. There are days when everything I plan falls into place exceptionally well and I leave school at the end of the day feeling like the best teacher ever to teach. On the flip side, there are days when the best-laid plans completely and utterly implode and the students practically rise up and unanimously convey that I am the worst teacher ever to teach.

Those are the times when I find myself dipping to emotional lows I never thought possible. The problem is that those really deep dark emotional feelings radiate from me for days at a time. My family became concerned and eventually so did I after being stubborn for nearly two quarters of the school year.

Often when media outlets run surveys regarding the most stressful occupations, the reigning champion for stress in almost every stress survey is that of a teacher.

Let me first convey the fact that I love the job of teaching high school. For as long as I can remember I have always loved working with kids. For the longest time that took the form of coaching and organizing special programs. It has always been what I aspired to do in life. I have also enjoyed dabbling in the world of entrepreneurship for profit and not for profit that connected around families or kids.

I have been a teacher in the Rockford public school system for ten years now and have enjoyed teaching nearly the entire time. For the last five years I have proudly taught at Rockford East High School, from where coincidently I graduated in 1978.

The day-to-day challenges I face in an inner-city public school are much like those of any other teacher. As the teacher of business and computer electives, the ongoing challenge of convincing students that electives are as important as any core curriculum class continues to be a difficulty.

By March 31, 2008, when the heart attack took place, I had created classes that were full of really awesome kids. I teach mostly freshman, and normally the first three quarters of any year are spent convincing freshman that high school is indeed different from middle school when it comes to maturity and theoretically getting ready for adulthood upon graduating.

As the sequence of events unfolded on the day of my heart attack and I thought it was just a pinched nerve or a slipped disk in my back, I was very cognitive of students arriving at school and the fact that I had to "man up" and prepare for first hour as no substitute had been called for replacement. As my early students started to enter my room and sit down in assigned seats as the first and tardy bells rang I felt an ever-greater need to "man up." I attempted to dry my ever-growing tears of pain as I did everything within me to mentally block out the searing shoulder blade pain.

As the students started to enter the classroom, Deanna, the

assistant principal, made the decision to first hold students outside of the classroom and then ultimately to move kids to the classroom next door to mine. I so badly wanted everything to return to normal as I desperately did not want to upset the conventional school day for the students.

About the time the ambulance gurney arrived in the classroom I finally accepted the fact that March 31 would not be a conventional day in my teaching career or for that matter in the rest of my life. As the EMTs rolled me down the hallway I hated the idea of students seeing me in a weak position but also the fact that some would think the worst and be very upset.

It was on the following day that I felt horrible about missing school and my students. I remember vividly wanting to get up and go to class. I found myself clock-watching as at what would have been first hour, 9:30 AM, I wondered to myself what the students were thinking about my situation.

I later found out that on both March 31 and April 1 there were quite a few kids who were very upset. As a lesson to be learned from my "event" I would hope that in the future the administration would deal proactively with each and every class that I taught and provide counseling now rather than assuming or presuming that kids are resilient, non-caring, or simply can handle the situation on their own.

The frustration I felt each and every day was huge as I struggled with not being at school on a daily basis and teaching like nothing had ever happened. As a teacher the students become an important factor in our lives. Teachers at some point begin, I think, to find the fountain of youth as a teacher. With the frustrations associated with teaching there also come incredible rewards and satisfaction. Turning off that emotional spigot is difficult at best.

The administration, staff, and teaching staff at East High School have been fantastic as I expected throughout the 2009 school year thus far. I think every teacher, both veterans of last year and newbies, has been told about March 31, 2008. I may sound a little neurotic, but I cannot help but feel that almost on a daily basis early in the year, some teacher, staff member, or school engineering staff (Charles) checked up on me in my room or called me by phone for what seemed to be a little thin reason at the time.

I am not sure of the date specifically, but it happened early in the school year when the appointed administrator walked by my classroom and looked through the small door window. Rose, the assistant principal at school, witnessed me with my head down on the desk table. As administrators normally do when they see me in the classroom, she opened the door and proceeded to make small talk and query me as to if everything was okay. Hearing no response from me regarding her query, Rose raised her voice and asked yet again. With both questions I failed to answer her query. Immediately, given my heart attack history, Rose thought I was dead or at the very least in the middle of another heart attack. Rose, doing her job as the professional she is, immediately picked up my classroom phone and called the main office to alert everyone that Mr. Fox was having another heart attack and that they should call 911. Understandably, her voice was emotional and at a rather high volume.

Immediately, after hearing the excited words and numbers of **heart attack and 911,** I jumped up, took off my iPod ear buds, stopped listening to Big and Rich, "Save a Horse (Ride a Cowboy)," and started running to the door to assist Rose with someone in grave immediate danger in the hallway.

After taking a few large steps toward the door, I looked quickly to Rose to ask where the person was having the heart attack. Before I was able to get the words out of my mouth, Rose looked at me with a high level of anguish. When I realized what I had done and why she was calling the office and 911, I too became very upset.

I am not sure if I had ever felt as bad as I did at the moment as my heart felt absolutely horrible as I could see that Rose was very upset and genuinely cared for me and my life. Quickly, Rose and I both realized that the office had started springing into action with the dialing of 911 due to the emergency policy of the school. It took several minutes for me to feel convinced that Rose's health was not at risk as a result of the unintentional scare I had given her.

Rose and I are able to laugh about the situation that transpired that day now, but I did promise her that it would be the last time I would wear an iPod and put my head down for the rest of my teaching career.

Teaching is a complicated and time-consuming profession that is not for everyone. While baby boomers remember the TV schools like *Welcome Back Kotter*, high school today is very different than generally remembered. The stress associated with teaching can be quite intense some days.

I don't think there exists a perfect high school where high students behave perfectly, technology works without complication all the time, and sufficient books are provided in a budget crisis. In my instance these rather lofty goals generally do not exist. The Rockford, Illinois, school district is the consummate inner-city public school. I would argue that in similar inner-city schools 90 percent of students are well behaved and 10 percent hate school, try to make it a free-for-all, and make the profession of being a teacher and loving it a consummate nightmare.

I would argue that there are two distinct groups of teachers. The first group of teachers is those who love to teach and generally aspire to provide the best education possible and ultimately fulfill the dreams and aspirations of their students. The other group of teachers does it for the money and benefits and generally does it because their summers are free and when they leave work every day they can just punch out and return the following day.

I, for one, anguish and internalize nearly each and every failure my students experience. I look at the student population as a large family. Perhaps I am in fact wrong in my feelings, but in a perfect world where teachers consider each student their own, failure should break their hearts much like it does mine.

Given that analogy, I find teaching to be a rather stressful job at the very least. Teaching is not a perfect science, and I probably am glad that it is not. I hate to see students fail, and more than anything else, I passionately hate to see them intentionally fail. The stress associated with teaching with a passion can be immense and at times numbing.

As much as I have attempted to stay positive and continue to forge forward, this past year it has been difficult. The stress associated with teaching after a heart attack is not what I would call a great idea. The fact of the matter is that I love teaching and working with kids. I have found myself this year putting a lid on my "up" passion but more importantly trying to put a definable floor on my "down" emotional feelings and frustrations. The problem with that approach is that the students who generally excel will probably not be pushed with excitement to loftier heights.

The recommendations that I would have for the recovering heart attack patient would be several in order to avoid work-related stress. I know my list does not include all stress-limiting factors, but hopefully my list will provide a mental stimulus for others.

- Try to get the textbooks or specified educational materials your class needs.

- Avoid shooting from the hip with vaguely designed class curriculum.
- Find a way to work with your administration to provide increased administrative support for that 10 percent of students who have no clue why they attend school.
- Determine the three or four "go to" students in each class who can support what you are doing and empower and challenge them to act as student presenters.
- Get organized and prepared for each and every day. Prepare for success mentally versus the alternative.
- Find those mental escape images and frame them in desktop frames.
- Use your cell phone or classroom computer to send an occasional text or e-mail to one of your family members. It can be short message like "How's life?"
- Find wall art that can provide a reminder of that "happy escape place"; for example, a large poster of the Iditarod dog race (okay, that works for me).

Regardless of what your profession or work is, my suggestions can be translated into job-specific points of your own.

Since my heart attack I have found the therapeutic need to create those life experiences that I still would like to accomplish as I search out the best way to minimize stress in my day-to-day life. I would encourage every heart attack patient to search their inner dreams and aspirations and put a life list together. The need for family input is critical in putting together the "living list" and as a brainstorming basis.

Keep in mind that your world as a heart attack victim is dramatically different from that of your family members or loved ones. It is not that you don't love them and appreciate their input, but feelings associated with suffering a heart attack are at best difficult to communicate or complicated to explain.

Don't feel selfish about your list; rather get excited about it. On those days when my classroom is rather difficult, I find myself mentally planning for one item off of the living list or perhaps contemplating adding additional experiences to the list.

Living List:

- *Throw out first pitch and sing during seventh-inning stretch at a Chicago Cubs game*

- *www.chicago.cubs.mlb.com*

- *Watch start of Iditarod dog sled race www.iditarod.com*

- *Ride horse in Cheyenne Frontier Days Parade www.cfdrodeo.com*

- *Go on Alaskan cruise*

- *Ride horse on pathway to Gettysburg battleground*

- *http://www.visit-gettysburg.com/gettysburg-horseback-riding.html*

- *Co-star in western movie … okay … a bit part*

- *Ride Outlaw Trail Ride—Thermopolis, Wyoming www. rideoutlawtrail.com*

- *Set* Guinness Book of World Records *record for world's largest 10,000-person, 5-mile trail ride for heart attack survivors and loved ones*

- *Watch the nightly ceremony and fireworks at Mount Rushmore … again www.travelsd.com/placestogo/rushmore/*

- *Cabin-to-cabin dogsled trip in Ely, Mn.*

- *http://www.ely.org/winter/winter_news.php?a=packages*

My son's letter

CHAPTER 22

The one-year anniversary of my heart attack has quickly passed, and East High School has just hosted the third annual Disney Days at Rockford East High School. I take special pride in this event, as we are the only high school in the state of Illinois that Walt Disney World visits to recruit promising high school graduating seniors.

Stephanie, Dad, and Brandon at Disney World

I guess opportunities like providing a springboard opportunity for graduating seniors with such a world-renowned company are perhaps just why I became a teacher. Reading everything I can about the life and times of Walter Elias Disney and what he stood for in his life I discover much of what I too feel is important to personal development.

The opportunity that the Disney Company gave my son is something that I think will forever pay dividends in his life. Getting into the Disney College Program and prospering in it is something that will pay personal dividends for his entire life as he moves up the corporate ladder at Disney Company.

The words my son used to convey his feelings to Disney regarding my new Disney shirt being cut off by the emergency room staff conveyed the emotions and words that Walt probably would have used if he were thrust into the same situation.

Suffice it to say that on the day my son was to return to Orlando after helping me through the weeks between my heart attack and his return trip two months later, a special father/son moment occurred that makes me emotional to this day.

Just hours before his departure time, a UPS truck pulled up to Dakota High School and delivered a box. Within moments of the UPS truck leaving, my son and wife brought me the package that UPS had delivered. Upon opening the box I don't think I have ever felt emotionally like I did at that moment. I was at a total loss for words. I was in shock, as I never expected that shirt to return. I hugged my son for what seemed like only seconds as he prepared to leave.

I learned later that I had not even said "thank you" to my son, as my wife told me after he left. For the next several hours I felt horrible, until I was able to call him upon his flight landing in Orlando. That night, just before I slept, I cried with happiness for the first time.

The truly Disney moment about the entire day was that in my son's haste to complete the letter requesting the replacement of the cut shirt he had inadvertently forgotten to provide a return address for the response from Disney. I am sure it was a devoted Disney cast member who took the extra time to locate him, but many companies would not have made that effort to respond.

How that empowered cast member learned that Dakota High School even existed or the coincidence that my wife taught high school at Dakota we probably will never know. Walter Elias Disney himself would have been proud of that Disney cast member who provided for the timely Disney touch.

One-year anniversary

The arrival of the anniversary of March 31, 2008, was in some ways more difficult than other anniversaries that I have encountered. There were parts of me that looked at the cup as if it were half empty and thought about March 31, 2008, as the worst day of my life. That part of my consciousness found me despising and hating the idea that I had ever experienced the heart attack.

It was during my first meeting with Dr. Kim Lebowitz at Northwestern University Hospital at the Bluhm Cardiovascular Institute that I took a major emotional step. I always responded to people by reflecting on the unfortunate luck of my heart attack and why I survived the heart attack and responding to their questions by saying, "It was because I am supposed to someday win the mega-lottery."

It was Dr. Lebowitz who put everything for me in perspective when she responded that "perhaps on March 31 you did in fact win the lottery." Since our meeting I have considered her posed question and discovered that yes in fact I did.

The other part of me looking at the cup as half full firmly thought that March 31, 2008, was the luckiest day of my life. There were so many things that had to happen in coordination with each other in order for me to be alive today. If any of these events failed to happen, all other events would have been irrelevant and would have only been another moment in time.

- The heart attack could have happened while I was throwing hay or chain-sawing trees, but I had to be at the school, as it was located three minutes from the hospital, versus at home thirty-five minutes from the hospital.
- The school administrator had to stop by the classroom versus a conventional day of not stopping by at that time of the morning; otherwise my stubbornness would have precluded my living.
- If the event happened any other time of the day the administrators and nurse would have been kept busy by student demands.
- If my heart attack had happened two weeks earlier when tardy policies were lax, the rear parking lot would have been congested and the ambulance would have never gotten close to its needed location for quick action.
- If my heart attack had waited until later in the day when students filled the hallway, the EMTs would have never had quick access to my room.
- The day-to-day functioning of the school elevator is generally considered hit and miss. Without a fully functional elevator that day, I would have died while waiting for the elevator or while getting bumped down the stairs on a gurney.
- East High School is only three minutes and twenty seconds from Swedish American Hospitals. All other high schools are

located further from any other hospital. If I were in one of those schools teaching I would have died in transit.

- I am not sure if there is a medical protocol related to how many times a heart attack patient is shocked back to life, but on my day, when my heart refused to keep beating, doctors at Swedish American refused to lose hope and stop shocking at five times as that would have left me dead. Going to six times gave me a chance to live.

To this day, it is difficult for me to consider just how lucky I am as a heart attack victim. The coordination of events was what I would consider a miracle. To consider how all the events had to occur in progression with each other is something Las Vegas would never put odds on, with all events happening as they did that very special day in March.

As I conveyed at the beginning of this book, it was my intention to provide the heart attack victim with a roadmap to recovery. It was of equal importance that I also provide the loved one a similar roadmap into what might be the emotional and physical path to recovery.

I am pretty sure that the vast majority of victims and loved ones will not be placed in the situation that I experienced in June facing the implementation of plan B on a horse, but I would suggest that at some point the victim will need to face a "moment" where they feel the need to prove "I still can."

Moving Forward

Chapter 24

All heart attacks are not created equal or for that matter are not even similar, as I have learned. I have come to realize that it is not how the heart attack arrives that really matters; it is instead what the patient does with the really difficult situation that counts. The emotional and physical challenges the heart disease patient faces will be incredibly daunting at times. They will often feel very alone and misunderstood by those who have never felt the physical and mental pain and anguish of suffering through a devastating heart attack.

Friends and loved ones, I have learned, will do everything possible to better understand what the victim is experiencing in order to help. And they should! Even with all their efforts to listen and understand, and those of the heart patient to explain the nuances of surviving a heart attack, the loved ones will really never completely understand, because ultimately no words fully describe the heart attack experience.

This book is written with all the ups and downs that I have faced in the last twelve months since my heart attack. Family and loved ones should have a better roadmap of what might be happening or what might still happen to the heart attack victim after reading this book.

The day-to-day life of a heart attack patient can be described much like that of a roller-coaster. The mind and body has been through a very traumatic event that should not be underestimated or minimized. The heart attack patient desperately wants to return to what used to be a normal existence and live a normal life.

The psychological roller-coaster combined with the physical roller-coaster related to prescription drugs and occasional chest tinges only add to the emotional frustrations of the heart patient.

I would suggest that loved ones or friends do what they can to engage the mind and if possible the body of the heart attack patient. Provide them with a reason to get out of the house and be active whenever possible. Find a local sporting event at a high school or college to watch as there is bound to be some game going on year round. If there is availability in the community, a light-hearted play or perhaps a musical, an amateur or professional type of activity, might just do the trick. I would suggest perhaps a good movie, but make sure it is not a downer, as that is the last thing a heart patient needs.

Don't be afraid to engage the heart patient in a board game that everyone can play as a family. There are always clubs or activities at the local college or university that perhaps might be of interest to get involved in. Take the time to listen and then engage in conversation.

Take the time to explore with the patient what might be involved in accomplishing something on the "Living List." Don't be negative about their "Living List." It is their "Living List" and not yours. Get them thinking about their "Living List" and how much fun it would be to fulfill.

If the heart attack survivor is unable to power-walk so they can start rebuilding them self physically, get them to at least start walking along a river or perhaps through a park. Keep the mood relaxed and fun. Walking with them is not the time to drop all the bad news the world has to offer.

If I were to suggest a few thing to the family and loved ones, it would be to keep an open mind, don't be judgmental regarding how much effort the victim is making to recover, and take time to listen; but more than anything else, don't ignore or forget that someone they love or care for has been through something very difficult and always understand the emotional roller-coaster they are more than likely experiencing. Don't ever forget that you're not the only one who wants life to be normal again.

If there was one objective or goal that all impacted by the heart attack experience should pursue from the earliest moment possible it is their one special thing. Work individually or together, but find just one thing. Find your SpectroMagic moment, special song, special cause, special project, special vacation, or anything else that sends tingles down the heart patient's spine and brings a smile to the very heart of the recovering heart attack patient. When that special occasion is realized, only then will the recovery begin in earnest.

To this day I firmly believe that I was blessed on March 31, 2008. I believe I was given that luck for some special reason. Perhaps that special reason is writing this book. If I am able to bring comfort, hope, and a greater understanding of heart attacks to loved ones and heart attack patients then I am living today for a valid reason.

CPSIA information can be obtained
at www.ICGtesting.com
Printed in the USA
LVHW110948040922
727581LV00005B/131